Henry James at Work

Henry James at Work

by *Theodora Bosanquet*

WITH EXCERPTS FROM HER DIARY AND AN
ACCOUNT OF HER PROFESSIONAL CAREER

EDITED WITH NOTES AND INTRODUCTIONS BY
Lyall H. Powers

THE UNIVERSITY OF MICHIGAN PRESS
Ann Arbor

Copyright © 2006 by Lyall H. Powers
All rights reserved
Published in the United States of America by
The University of Michigan Press
Manufactured in the United States of America
♾ Printed on acid-free paper

2009   2008   2007   2006   4   3   2   1

A CIP catalog record for this book is available from the British Library.

Library of Congress Cataloging-in-Publication Data

Bosanquet, Theodora.
    Henry James at work / by Theodora Bosanquet ; with excerpts from
her diary and an account of her professional career ; edited with
notes and introductions by Lyall H. Powers.
        p.   cm.
    ISBN-13: 978-0-472-11571-6 (cloth : alk. paper)
    ISBN-10: 0-472-11571-5 (cloth : alk. paper)
      1. James, Henry, 1843–1916.   I. Powers, Lyall H.   II. Title.
PS2123.B6   2006
813'.4—dc22
[B]   2006020164

For Loretta

AND IN HOMAGE TO LEON EDEL

(1907–1997)

Preface

Theodora Bosanquet is hardly a household name familiar to most educated readers. For that matter, Henry James is now scarcely less unfamiliar; and the book she wrote about him, *Henry James at Work*, is recognized only by the learned few. But who among them has actually read it? Henry James (1843–1916) is, of course, arguably the most accomplished author to be produced in the United States of America, a novelist and short story writer, theoretic and practical critic, dramatist and travel writer. *Henry James at Work* is a slim volume published by Leonard and Virginia Woolf at their Hogarth Press, London, in 1924. The author was a youthful woman of forty-four and, in spite of her rather arresting name, of solid English background—

> whom England bore, shaped, made aware,
> Gave, once, her flowers to love, her ways to roam,
> A body of England's breathing English air—

and properly educated in good English schools. She spent the last eight years of Henry James's life (called "the Major Phase" by old Jamesians) as his amanuensis, chiefly at Lamb House, down in Rye (East) Sussex, near the Channel Coast, and finally at 21 Carlyle Mansions on the north bank of the Thames in London.

James's need of secretarial assistance arose, early in 1897, with the onset of "writer's cramp"—now called "carpal tunnel syndrome." He first employed a particularly dour Scot named Macalpine to take his dictation in shorthand and then provide a typed copy; but, finding him too expensive and singularly unresponsive to the material being dictated, James decided he wouldn't do. James was then composing "The Turn of the Screw," in which his technique was intended to make his readers "think the evil for themselves" (and there was an abundance of opportunity for that); Macalpine evidently thought nothing at all. He was replaced at the turn of the century. Mary Weld from the Secretarial Bureau of Miss Mary Petherbridge, in London, moved into the vacancy and served until August 1904, when James left for the United States. Weld married soon after. James tried others, but none really satisfied until the advent of Theodora Bosanquet.

The need was urgent: James had embarked on the exhausting project of reviewing and revising his prose works—novels and stories—for a "definitive edition" to be published by Scribner's in twenty-three volumes (December 1907–July 1909, it grew to twenty-four), in evident emulation of Balzac's twenty-three-volume *Comédie humaine*. Into that demanding chore Miss Bosanquet was immediately launched—and gratefully. The experience would urge and foster her own nascent literary career. She soon began contributing items to the *Saturday Westminster Gazette,* coauthored a novel published before James's death (February 1916), and would complete, a few months later, the first of three major essays on Henry James, her "own great Man."[1] A year later she completed the second, and at the end of 1920, the third. These formed the basis for her memoir *Henry James at Work.*

The little book emphasized the "spiritual" quality of James as an author, his indebtedness to an inspirational force very like the poet's muse; James called it "my good angel"—*mon bon ange,* usually shortened to the familiar "mon bon." Bosanquet makes a strong case in favor of the author's revised versions of his fictions as superior to the originals. She recognizes clearly the "difficulty" of James's late style—and sometimes vigorously castigates it (in the privacy of her personal diary)—but defends it intelligently in *Henry James at Work.* The argument she persuasively presents is that the revisions regularly result in a more lifelike depiction of characters, settings, and actions, and therefore a more significant, more *meaningful* realism. With that, the

---

1. See Diary A, entry for 12 December 1907.

Bosanquet kept a single diary during her years with James and after. I have, however, arranged entries quoted according to topics into three groups here and called them Diary A—on Bosanquet's professional relationship with James and his family and a few friends; Diary B—on her literary taste and affiliations; and Diary C—on her interest in psychic phenomena. The entries in each grouping are given in chronological order. I make a few references to entries not reproduced here. The diary manuscript is in the Houghton Library of Harvard University.

revised version sharpens the important distinction between telling and showing, presentation and representation: lifelikeness depends on the quality of self-containment in fiction that is able to stand on its own, apparently free of the author's controlling hand. James's art (Theodora insists) enabled him to exhibit life dramatically and so to transmit the convincing look of life—"the look that conveys its meaning." A convincing and *original* critical perception. It is perhaps the originality of Theodora Bosanquet's acute critical observations that will most urgently grasp readers of *Henry James at Work*.

Acknowledgments

First, my thanks to Leon Edel, who originally proposed the new edition of *Henry James at Work* to me as a joint venture, rather like our edition of *The Complete Notebooks of Henry James*. He had arranged for publication by the French house Les Editions du Seuil, in Paris. (We of
course expected an English edition to follow as well, by and by.) The
plan, as far as it went, was that Edel would write an Introduction,
largely a reminiscence of Theodora Bosanquet, whom he had known
for many years. At his death in September 1997, Edel left a few scraps
of notes for the project and a paragraph or two of his reminiscence of
Theodora Bosanquet; I undertook to provide a substitute Introduction
and in Edel's idiom—as far as that was possible. Editions du Seuil published *Henry James à l'ouvrage* in 2000, and the present volume is the
anticipated English Edition, much enlarged—particularly by a supple-
mental and compensatory section "Theodora Bosanquet at Work."

I am grateful to the director and staff of the Houghton Library at
Harvard University. I am likewise grateful for the kindness of the staff
of the Hatcher Library in the University of Michigan: Peggy E. Daub
(Head of Department of Rare Books and Special Collections), Kathryn
L. Beam (Senior Associate Librarian, Humanities Curator), Joanne E.
Spaide (Supervisor, Information Resources), and Thomas C. Burnett
(Information and Resource Specialist). My thanks go to the staff of the
University of Michigan Press as well—Erica Bollerud for assistance in
preparing the original manuscript and Rebecca Mostov for broad general management of the final text; my amazed gratitude to Richard
Isomaki for sharp-eyed and keenly intelligent scrutiny of proof and to
Marcia LaBrenz for unflagging attention to all the details of copyedit-
ing; and my heartfelt thanks to the wise LeAnn Fields for her benevolent advice and guidance through this whole undertaking. Finally, I
am, as always, happy to thank my wife, Loretta, for her persistent sage
counsel and unselfish support.

Contents

Introduction

Fate seems to have been responsible for the coming together of Theodora Bosanquet and Henry James in the late summer of 1907, fate or James's guardian angel, *mon bon*. Perhaps it was the combination of fate, breeding, and personal preparation judiciously intermingled. Before the end of the nineteenth century, Bosanquet had been introduced to James's fiction: as a pre-teenager she had happened upon a copy of *The Europeans* in her father's study; a few years later, before she had turned twenty, a friend had lent her a copy of *The Two Magics*—one of which was the engaging "The Turn of the Screw." That introduction inevitably led her to further immersion into James's work, including that of his "Major Phase"—and especially the rich and challenging *The Ambassadors* (1903).

As for breeding—she was born on 3 October 1880, at Sandown (now Sandown-Shanklin) on the lovely Isle of Wight, and from the sturdy Huguenot stock of her father, Frederick C. T. Bosanquet. The family called her "Dora." An adjacent branch of the family included the noted philosopher Bernard Bosanquet (1843–1923; of University College, Oxford), and his impressive array of brothers—Admiral Sir Day A. Bosanquet; Robert Holford Bosanquet F.R.S., Fellow of St. John's College, Oxford; and Charles Bosanquet, a founder and first secretary of the Charity Organisation Society. Theodora's mother, Gertrude Mary née Fox, was descended from a branch of the Darwin family. Gertrude's mother was the daughter of the Reverend William Darwin Fox (1805–80), a grandson of William Alvey Darwin (1726–83). That Darwin was an older brother of Erasmus, five years his junior. Erasmus was a physician, a scientist, an influential poet among the early Romantics, and an inventor like his American friend Benjamin Franklin, with whom he was allied in support of the American Revolution. Erasmus (1731–1802) was perhaps the most accom-

plished of all the Darwins, including his famous grandson Charles (of
The Origin of Species). One of William Alvey's daughters married a
Fox; the resulting son, William Darwin Fox, was not only a second
cousin of *the* Charles Darwin (1809–82), but also his most intimate
and enduring friend during their years at Cambridge and onward.
Both young men were talented naturalists, but cousin Fox prepared
for the clergy and upon graduation accepted a parish on the Isle of
Wight. That relationship continued, and Theodora Bosanquet's diary
entry for 13 April 1915 records her "going to supper at Hornton
Street, where Uncle Ras was staying, very large and tactless and
grumbly, as usual." This was Erasmus the grandson of Charles-the-
Famous, son of his second-youngest son, Horace, and thus a cousin
rather than "Uncle" and also a year younger than Theodora. Ras was
killed in action that year.

The Darwin connection necessarily allied Theodora with the
equally prominent Wedgwoods, potters of Staffordshire. *Pater familias*
Erasmus Darwin was a close friend of master potter Josiah Wedgwood
I. The two shared cultural and political tastes: both sympathized
wholeheartedly with the French Revolution; both were abolitionists.
Josiah's renowned cameo depicting a black slave kneeling under the
legend "Am I not a man and a brother?" gives additional significance to
his regular donations to the Society for Abolishing the Slave Trade.

The descendants of these two stalwarts were further allied by a
steady practice of intermarriage. Josiah Wedgwood I married Sarah,
née Wedgwood; both direct descendants of their common great-
great-grandfather, Gilbert Wedgwood (1588–1678). Their first
daughter, Susannah, married Erasmus Darwin's son Robert; their
children included Caroline and Charles. Susannah's brother Josiah
Wedgwood II and his wife produced a daughter, Emma. Caroline
married her cousin Josiah III; Charles married his cousin Emma, who
was thus also niece of her mother-in-law. A close-knit family, you
might say. It is tempting to consider that this intensely intermixed sib-
linghood encouraged the humanitarian emphasis that characterized the
policies of the Darwin-Wedgwood clan.

Another connection of typical significance is the friendship of
Charles's older brother Ras (Erasmus) and Emma's older brother
Hensleigh Wedgwood; these cousins directed their benevolent atten-

tion to the prolific writer and somewhat eccentric feminist Harriet Martineau—daughter of a Huguenot surgeon. Martineau attracted the notice of the cousins and also of Hensleigh's wife, Fanny (née Mackintosh). All three were close contemporaries. The two men were especially alert to Martineau's material welfare. A confirmed bachelor and fashionable *cavaliere servente,* Ras had alarmed his Darwin siblings Caroline and Charles by his constant waiting upon Miss Harriet in London at all hours. Her letters repeatedly thank him for gifts—"books, champagne, and oysters and keeping him informed of her physical symptoms and financial status."[1] Ras had offered to have a room added to the invalided Martineau's dwelling at Tynemouth (1840–44). He and Hensleigh had succeeded in procuring a testimonial fund for her, and the cousins became joint treasurers thereof. Harriet Martineau's influence in the family—as associated feminist, abolitionist, and practicing mesmerist—extended well beyond just Darwins and Wedgwoods and on into the Bosanquets.

So much, then, for breeding—and now the matter of personal preparation. Bosanquet's formal education placed her at the forefront of feminist progress (or at least endeavor) in England and into the ranks of the suffragists (soon to be suffragettes). She attended one of the very earliest educational institutions for female students in England, the Cheltenham Ladies College, founded in 1853; only the North London Collegiate School (1850) was earlier.[2] She was then graduated, B.Sc., from University College, the University of London. The professions were mainly closed to women as the nineteenth century yielded to the twentieth: at her death in 1876, Harriet Martineau had been the only regular female journalist in the country. Would such a career be open to the young Miss Bosanquet?

In any case, Bosanquet continued her preparation by enrolling, at the beginning of 1907, in the Secretarial Bureau of Miss Mary Petherbridge in Conduit Street in London, "where young women were taught typewriting and shorthand and everything else secretaries

---

1. Harriet Martineau, *Selected Letters,* ed. Valerie Sanders (Oxford: Clarendon Press, 1990), xxiv.
2. Margaret Haig Thomas, Lady Rhondda, *Leisured Women,* Hogarth Essays, 2nd series, 11 (London: Hogarth Press, 1928), 15.

should know, although her own dominant interest was the art and craft of indexing."[3] Bosanquet's reminiscence continues:

> I had moved [from indexing records of the East India Company]. . . . The Report of the Royal Commission on Coast Erosion was engaging my eyes and pen. Suddenly the pen stopped writing and my eyes leapt to a little table at the end of the room where a girl sitting in front of a typewriter was grappling with words read slowly from a book. . . . I sat and stared. Why were those passages from *The Ambassadors* being dictated? . . . When my bewilderment broke into a question I was told that Mr. Henry James wanted an amanuensis.

Bosanquet made further enquiries of Miss Petherbridge, who could hardly believe that anyone trained in the art and craft of indexing could possibly be interested—the young woman at the table certainly wasn't—but arranged to let Bosanquet be interviewed. "On 22 August Henry James came to see what Miss Petherbridge had to offer him. . . . He said he would find rooms where I could be lodged and fed. We could start in October." They did, just a week after Bosanquet's twenty-seventh birthday. Would she suit?

A week later, Henry James wrote to his brother William to announce that he was safely returned to London with "a new excellent amanuensis from thence, a young boyish Miss Bosanquet, who is worth all the other (females) that I have had put together. . . . There is no comparison!"[4] The term "amanuensis" perhaps needs a word of explanation: Bosanquet and James used it almost exclusively to refer to her position. It means "a person who takes dictation or copies something already written"—a kind of handmaid. Bosanquet was careful to explain, many years later, the distinction they observed between the terms *amanuensis* and *secretary*. To answer a query from biographer Leon Edel about whether James usually had a screen around his typist (which Edel doubted), Bosanquet wrote,

3. Theodora Bosanquet, "As I Remember—Henry James," *Time and Tide,* 3 July 1954, 875.
4. Letter from Lamb House, Rye, dated 17 October 1907 (*Henry James: Letters,* ed. Leon Edel IV [1895–1916], Cambridge: Harvard University Press, 1984). First part ends, "I must go to bed and finish tomorrow!" The continuation, dated 18 October, contains the Bosanquet reference.

[T]here was certainly no screen around me and I never heard of one. But I was warned by Miss Petherbridge . . . that he liked his amanuensis to be detached and occupied. . . . I didn't stitch or knit myself, but kept a book open and read it. Sometimes H.J. took a look at the open page and occasionally commented . . . he liked to come and take a look at the lines just typed sometimes.[5]

Bosanquet was comfortably enough settled in Mrs. Holland's just around the corner at the top of Mermaid Street, maybe thirty meters from the front door of Lamb House. She had friends in Rye, such as Nellie Bradley; Nellie was the daughter of James's Rye walking companion Arthur Granville Bradley (1850–1943), a travel writer especially on Canada and the state of Virginia, who lived in the accommodating Red Cottage on the north edge of Rye. Other friends were Rose Macaulay, Clara Smith, and Naomi Royde Smith. With some of these friends Bosanquet dabbled, somewhat seriously, in the occult, tarot cards and Ouija boards, spiritualism, and psychic phenomena. When William James visited Rye she was delighted to meet and talk with him on spiritualism and "modern psychology," and was knowing enough to ask intelligent questions and keep up her end of the conversations. She would later pursue those questions further, and with increased sophistication. Royde Smith became general editor of the Saturday Westminster Gazette, a prolific writer of novels, and the hostess of a modest literary salon; she encouraged Bosanquet to pursue her own budding literary career, especially her happy faculty with parody—and she did several of these on Henry James. A good example of Bosanquet's talent is one published in the Gazette on 23 January 1915, p. 10, under the title "Afterwards" (and another of these is discussed below in"The Hand-printed Hogarth Essay").

---

5. Theodora Bosanquet to Leon Edel, 13 October 1952. She had responded to an earlier question from Edel about a letter from James to G. B. Shaw concerning the play *The Saloon:* "He didn't keep copies of dictated letters. You see I wasn't a stenographer [one who takes down dictation in shorthand and later transcribes it in typewriting], so I didn't have a notebook—unfortunately. I could just tap out things on the typewriter but shorthand I never learnt and in fact H.J. didn't like or want a silent machine to dictate to. And I never used a carbon sheet except for the final copy of a play or novel" (21 November 1935).

AFTERWARDS

We print one of the parodies left over from last week, with a query as to the likelihood of any two characters imagined by the writer "E.R.M." has chosen to imitate so far forgetting themselves as to ride outside an omnibus.

Out of the so complex—the, to him, even unassimilable—mass of facts that London presented to him—thrust, as it were, before his vision to take or leave (but to take was an inevitable, a foredoomed compulsion since here he, so to speak, was)—the emergence of a certain exterior brilliance, a scintillation, a radiance almost too crudely illumining, if not values, anyhow the facts themselves, struck on him.

"One does, as it were, anyhow, so very immediately see!" he murmured; and till then had scarcely been aware how, in the near past, one had so very indubitably not seen.

To the further question, flung at him by the full glance of his companion's challenging eyes, "*What,* then, does one see?" he presented a baffled dubiety.

"In the last resort it must, you know, depend on who one is!"

She pursued him with, "And who, in the last resort, *are* we?"

He ever so faintly grimaced. "Oh, as to that!"

Then the so vivid external brilliance illumined even his thoughts to a certain careful lucidity.

"Aren't we," he speculated, "divided, as it were, roughly, into 'sorts'? Isn't the distinguishing feature of each 'sort' precisely the quantity and quality of its susceptibility to impulse?"

Her eyes threw at him, "Oh, you've, for once, quite too wonderfully 'got it!'"

He, believing himself to have ever so often "got it" before, was yet stimulated, even to garrulity, by the unattenuated fineness of her so rare recognition.

"So, then, the question emerges, what, from this particular motive force, is the quality of the impulse to which we each are susceptible? Where is it, so to speak, 'landing us'?" He waved a hand over the newly visible city, quite obviously in the process of being "landed" on even too many shores simultaneously.

A flock of young men and women walked by, arm, almost unobtrusively, in arm. "Reactionary impulsion," he said (oh, he was thinking it all out), "the increased fervour of propinquity in the long forcibly detached."

Tentatively she indicated to him another two, promenading with faces averted and cold.

"?" she queried.

"Responsive impulsion. The enforced separation of the sexes voluntarily continued. There we have illustrated," he carried it on, "two of the three sections of people to which I (or didn't I?) alluded. One calls them, possibly, Respondents or Reactors. The sex thing, a small thing in itself"—(he thought so; he was wrong)—"typifies the whole network of actions, reactions and counteractions in which the world, so inextricably, is involved. The motive force to which we, ever so remotely, are referring has its Respondents and its Reactors, hasn't it, 'all over the place.' Only look," he illustrated, "at literature. As, a short time since, we had everywhere that phenomenon the writer turned fighter, so we have not the fighter turned writer again. With what results? A rough third of the new literature is saturated with the battle atmosphere: either the orange of the war-like is squeezed dry for our edification (largely by those who have stayed at home), or men and women write, indeed, of other things, but with the suddenness, the virility, the force, the colour of swords beaten into pens. Another third of the new literature is produced by the Reactors—those who have had, for long, too much war and rumours of war. . . ."

Oh, she knew that literature; even herself she produced it.

"But aren't there," she pondered lucidly, "three thirds in a whole?"

His eyes reproached her. "Wasn't I, my dear, coming to that? Listen!" His gesture indicated to what she was to listen. From the seat behind them (for they rode on a shrapnel-scarred 'bus) voices said, one to the other: "Those collars at Bourne's, they've gone down to one eleven three"; and "Only fancy!"

"Aren't you," he murmured, "'onto it' now? The immense array of the Indifferents, the immobile, the unsusceptible to impulsion. There you have your remaining (to put it at a low minimum) third. To them the war, quite magnificently, wasn't; the new world for all its obtrusiveness, its clamorous insistence, splendidly isn't. In the streets boys shouted a while ago, 'Destruction of Louvain,' 'Advance of Russians, Prussians, or Allies,' as the case might (or mightn't) be; as to-night they even raucously shout 'Capital Punishment for notorious editor and three M.P.'s,' 'Lord Southbeach to be President of German Republic,' 'End of Party System; establishment of the new'—was it Democracy or Autocracy? My hearing failed . . . well, it quite extraordinarily doesn't matter which. The answer from our friends behind (unless, indeed, they hear of an event in close propinquity or with touching details, when they may say, 'Killing babies! It does seem cruel!') is, merely, 'Those collars at Bourne's . . .' What has war been, with them, 'up to'? What has it, even remotely, taught them? Not life in the trenches, for they have stayed, quite solidly, in houses; not geography, for they have used neither maps nor flags; not knitting, for they, quite often, knitted before; not to preserve their lives in unlit streets, for they were, so one gathered from those sources unquenched by Censors, 'done in' in thousands; not even a healthy skepticism, for they will believe, in their unmoved fashion, everything (not excluding Russians) that they read in print. They are of an immobility . . ."

"And how," she said (oh, she had been thinking for herself, and not listening), "will the war affect class distinctions?"

His glance shamed her in consequence. "One doesn't," he gently put it, "jump so." "I was," she excused herself, "wondering; because, whereas I read somewhere that it would 'level the barriers between man and man,' a subaltern told me yesterday that it would 'put a stopper on all this beastly democracy.' Which, if either, had 'got there'?"

"Both," he adjudicated. "For what one finds must, in the last resort, so very precisely depend on what one is looking for. And there," he summed it up, "we are."

And there they, quite incontrovertibly, were.[6]

-E.R.M.[7]

---

6. The seasoned reader will detect, in that concluding sentence, a distinct enough echo of the conclusion of The Awkward Age (1899)—

She [Nanda Brookenham] faltered, but at last brought it out. "Yes. Do you see? There I am."

"I see. There we are. Well," said Mr. Longdon—"tomorrow."—

and also the conclusion of The Ambassadors (1903)—

She [Maria Gostrey] sighed it at last all comically, all tragically, away. "I can't indeed resist you."

"Then there we are!" said Strether.

7. The initials are a pseudonymous camouflage for the modest Bosanquet.

Coincidentally, Nellie Bradley suggested (on 13 January 1915, according to Bosanquet's diary) that Clara Smith collaborate with Bosanquet on a novel written in letters. The suggestions quickened their enthusiasm. The two authors began exchanging letters by their fictional characters. The Bosanquet diary for 17 January 1915 has this report: "I spent most of my energy during the week writing the first letter from 'Nicolas Romer' to his sister 'Mrs. Wychwood.' I found it the greatest fun to be writing as a single man living in a house in Cheyne Row and describing the visit of the terrible 'Miss Craske' bent on finding out the address, in Italy, of my sister and step-sister." The completed venture is stylistically a combination of James's epistolary stories "A Bundle of Letters" (1879), "The Point of View," (1882), and his related novel *The Awkward Age* (1898–99). The preface James provided for that novel to fit into the New York Edition illustrated his plan (and its relation to the two stories): "I drew on a sheet of paper . . . the neat figure of a circle consisting of a number of small rounds disposed at equal distance about a central object. The central object was my situation . . . and the small rounds represented so many distinct lamps, . . . the function of each of which would be to light with all intensity one of its aspects . . ."[8] James B. Pinker, Henry James's literary agent, had been, since 1913, Bosanquet's as well, and he negotiated a handsome contract with Constable & Co., London. She and Clara were exuberant. Their *Spectators* was published in 1916.

James's seriously failing health at the close of 1915 meant a great deal of extra work for Bosanquet. The generally ungrateful response of brother William's widow, Alice, daughter Peggy, and son Harry managed to lighten her workload;[9] but her virtual discharge from the scene frustrated and saddened her in her close relationship to the septuagenarian. She was allowed to do a skillful bit of editing on James's last publication, a preface to Rupert Brooke's *Letters from America;* she was enlisted to assist Percy Lubbock in the preparation of an edition of James's letters, carefully selected by the Jameses; and she managed to prepare three memorable essays on her "great Man"—the third was

---

8. *The Novels and Tales of Henry James,* vol. 9, preface, xvi.
9. Widow Alice James et al. objected to the "intrusive" presence of TB in HJ's domicile—continuing the work (as secretary, etc.) that she (TB) was used to doing—and so lightened her work load. See Diary A for Thursday 16 December 1915, and for Saturday 8 January 1916.

published in 1920, the year Percy Lubbock's (and her) *The Letters of Henry James* appeared.

Bosanquet was also involved, during the last two years of World War I, as assistant in the "Who's Who" section of the War Trade Intelligence Department; during the following two years, 1918–20, she was assistant to the Secretary of the Ministry of Food. In 1919 she was decorated for her war work with an MBE. She was forty years old, and her future lay before her. *Henry James at Work* was published in 1924 and, slightly revised, in 1927; then, in the United States, in 1928, came a republication of the first edition—a very satisfying achievement. But much more remained. At the end of that decade a new Jamesian connection was created by a letter enquiring about her role as James's amanuensis; it came from a young man out of McGill University, Montreal, Canada—Leon Edel, beginning his lifelong scholarly engagement with Henry James. Bosanquet invited him to her office in Crosby Hall, Cheyne Walk, Chelsea, on 21 November 1929. Of course, he accepted, and that would begin another chapter, here called "Theodora Bosanquet at Work," below.

The Handprinted Hogarth Essay

Theodora Bosanquet's pamphlet *Henry James at Work* (London: Hogarth Press, 1924, rev. 1927) is a unique document in that it offers an account of Henry James, man and author, during the final stage of his life and career; it is an immediate and intimate account by an acute, sensitive witness of her experience gained at first hand. Theodora Bosanquet was closely associated with James during his last eight years, a brief period but an important one: he was then reviewing the fiction he had produced over the preceding forty-three years and revising those items he selected for inclusion in the New York Edition of his novels and tales. As his secretary she assisted, thus, in the review of that career and not only in the actual revision but also—if more briefly—in the difficult decision of which works to include and which to reject. She also participated in his creation of the very important series of prefaces for the edition. In consequence, she was a direct witness to a good deal of James's theoretic basis for his revisions, explicitly or implicitly expressed, and was thus enabled to speak with firmer conviction and stronger authority than many others on the principles involved.

Theodora Bosanquet was likewise privy to James's creation of new work—"inventive" work, he called it. Resumption of James's theatrical experiment gave her experience with the Jamesian "dramatic mode" under three distinct but interrelated headings: the creation of new plays, the transgeneric adaptation of fiction for theatrical production and vice versa, and, perhaps most important of all, the relation between Jamesian fiction and drama—or, more exactly, the fundamentally dramatic character and quality of James's literary works. And she similarly participated in his creation of new fiction and in his resumption of temporarily abandoned fiction, particularly *The Sense of the Past*. Her special position as amanuensis establishes her testimony as one of unparalleled authority.

Readers of this Hogarth essay ought always to be aware that Theodora Bosanquet's account depends on a breadth of firsthand experience; they may safely trust their sense that a great deal lies behind her specific observations. When she quotes (in sections IV and V of *Henry James at Work*) James's remarks in defense of revision—from the preface to *The Golden Bowl*—one can rest assured that she does so with extensive knowledge of all the preparation—the repondering and consequent oral rehearsal of ideas—that lay behind those remarks. Nor should readers doubt the impressive ring of authenticity in her account of the appearance and behavior of James the man and his peculiar practice as an artist.

Behind the accounts in *Henry James at Work* lies the corroborative testimony of the Bosanquet personal diaries, assiduously sustained throughout her association with the Master.[1] The diary entries always enrich the account of the published essay, and on some occasions they even add useful correction. Her brief recall of their quotidian regime is a case in point. Section IV indicates that her secretarial duties at Lamb House ran from 10:30 A.M. to 1:30 P.M. That was perhaps typical, but there were exceptions. Her diary entry for 5 January 1908 (she was near the end of her third month with him) records that James had not dictated more than five hundred words that morning, and observes, "It *is* a nice easy job and no mistake." But that was a *Sunday* morning, and the nice easy job frequently involved her attendance at Lamb House on all seven days of the week. Sometimes she was obliged to return to the Remington after tea (6:00 to 7:30 P.M.) and again after dinner (9:00 to 11:00 P.M.): the diary entries, for example, from Wednesday, 23 October 1907 through Sunday, 27 October 1907, when James was urgently converting his short story "Covering Eng" into the play *The High End*, indicate that she was thus on duty every evening except for Friday, 25 October—and that was when James was briefly in London. On that Saturday, the twenty-sixth, the diary informs us, James "produced chocolate soon after 10 and laid pieces beside me after carefully pulling off the silver paper." And on occasion

1. See "Excerpts from the Bosanquet Diary," in this volume, for illustrative diary entries.

James even dropped around at breakfast time to summon his amanuensis (she was just ten steps away, around the corner in Mermaid Street). Her first week's wages brought thirty-five shillings on 17 October 1907, "the first money I'd ever earned," she told him.[2]

Bosanquet soon proved herself an unusual secretary. During her first week she delighted James by mentioning that she had read his *The Tragic Muse* (her first task was taking his dictation of the preface to that novel): a week later she recorded his happy compliment:

At the close of the morning Mr. James said ". . . I have great pleasure in saying that I'm *extremely* satisfied, Miss Bosanquet. You seem to have picked things up so quickly and intelligently." I said I found it so interesting that it was only natural to do my best—and he said "among the faults of my previous amanuenses—not by any means the *only* fault—was their apparent lack of comprehension of what I was driving at"—so we parted quite pleased with each other. (Saturday, 19 October 1907)

In anticipation of an interval during which James would not need her services, she had asked him to provide her with a letter of recommendation. He responded, in May 1909, with this:

I have the greatest pleasure in testifying to my sense of the great ability and high values of Miss Theodora Bosanquet, acquired during two years of her constant, punctual and in every way faithful service with me as literary Secretary. I have the highest opinion of her intelligence, competence, alertness and discretion—her whole general accomplishment and character, to all of which I hope again frequently to resort for assistance. I have done highly important work—to myself—with her valuable aid, and shall cordially congratulate those who may enjoy it.

Bosanquet's account of James's practice of dictating his professional work and his letters (a practice which he had been following for some ten years before she came to him) is vivid and intelligent, and she sen-

---

2. Entry for Thursday, 17 October 1907. For a glimpse of her domestic regimen—bedtime, breakfast, etc.—see Diary A, 6, 7, 9 October 1914.

sibly explains the effect it had on his late style. That she was not always delighted with his habit of "breaking ground" preparatory to dictation of the actual novel itself is indicated in such a note as this of 1 November 1914 (a Sunday): "Mr. James started this morning on a long preliminary jawbation, to get himself worked up to the right pitch, about 'The Sense of the Past'" (Diary A). Yet *Henry James at Work* attests to her sympathetic understanding of the necessity, to James, of such careful preparation and of its contribution to the finished product.

At the end of section II Bosanquet's explanation of James's resorting to his pen, to "the manual labour of writing," when brevity and conciseness were at issue—for plays and short stories—leads to her interesting example of the preparation of his stories for his final collection: "It is almost literally true to say of the sheaf of tales collected in *The Finer Grain* that they were all written in response to a single request for a short story for *Harper's Monthly Magazine* . . . The tale eventually printed was Crapy Cornelia." A series of entries in the Bosanquet diary between November 1908 and January 1909 (Diary A) flesh out the background against which this drama was enacted—

26 November: "a frenzied morning of striving to 'boil down' 'The Tree Top'" [i.e., "The Top of the Tree," published as "The Velvet Glove" in *The English Review* in March 1909].

12 December: "Mr. James works steadily—at present on a quite short story for Harper's" ["Crapy Cornelia," published there in October 1909].

17 December: "Mr. James going on with 'short story' for Harper's which extends mightily—and is, I think, dull" ["Crapy Cornelia"].

2 January 1909: "Mr. James at work on another short story, which promises very well indeed" ["Mora Montravers," published in the *English Review*, August–September 1909].

3 January [Sunday]: "Mr. James had done a lot on his story last night and we raced along. He says he wants to do three or four, and finds his only plan is to write them himself—it keeps him more within bounds—and *then* dictate them."

8 January: "Mr. James began another story" ["The Bench of Desolation," published in *Putnam's* magazine, October–December 1910].

The role of the diaries in providing the broad general setting out of which *Henry James at Work* emerged establishes the importance of Bosanquet's evaluation of James's artistic practice and achievement. She was a young woman of intelligence and sure literary taste,[3] and although she was initially awed by her employer and admired him as man and artist, she was always capable of objectivity in her estimates of him—and even of stern disagreement (mainly, of course, confined to her diary) with him on some issues. She insisted, early and late, on the "greatness" of the Master. Her diary entry for 12 December 1907 contains a revealing combination of ideas; she has just begun reading Fanny Burney's diary:

> I had no idea it was so entertaining a book, and how it reflects on *me*—how little I have been able to put Mr. James on these pages. . . . Indeed these past days there has been nothing to relate of my own great Man, who paralyses me more and more. (Diary A)

Publication of Rebecca West's book *Henry James* (1916) gave Bosanquet the opportunity to reiterate her sense of his stature: "Rebecca West is liable to very vulgar lapses and . . . she's too intent on holding up H.J.'s limitations to view to lay enough stress on his greatness" (Diary B, 1 August 1916).

The diary resumes the theme of the Master's paralyzing effect— even when he is at his most gracious. On Bosanquet's return to Rye after a brief trip with her friend Clara Smith, James came around to hear of her travels, "but I don't think he can have found us very 'articulate' about them. I do wish he didn't paralyse me so much" (12 November 1913).[4] Yet she was mentally liberated enough, fundamentally, to keep her own thoughts and not yield to the opinions of her "own great Man." Her diary testifies to her sturdy-mindedness. Although she strives effectively, in *Henry James at Work,* to elicit our sympathetic understanding of James's late style, she was not always tolerant—privately—of his verbosity and long-windedness, the spilling over of his "jawbation." She complained to herself that James's

---

3. See Diary B, "Bosanquet's Literary Taste and Affiliations."
4. See Diary A, 22 March 1915, on James's similar "paralyzing" effect on Burgess Noakes, his valet.

letters have "so many superfluous words in them . . . and such a tremendous lot of abstract material" (24 March 1915). Throughout the weeks during which James resumed his work on *The Sense of the Past* the diary groans and grumbles over the wrong-headedness of the project. First, 4 November 1914—

> He began re-dictating it. At once there leaps up in me the old futile perverse objection to his *donnée*. . . . It seems to me a most absurd and unnecessary straining of the probabilities. . . . However! (Diary A)

Then on 13 January 1915, her doubts about the "essentially impossible idea" lead to the stern criticism that "he doesn't really face and solve his problems, anyway not his problems of possibility, he trusts to his technique to obscure the fact that they are there at all" (Diary A). And one of James's letters written to solicit funds for the American Volunteer Motor-Ambulance Corps (of which he was the English chairman) was bothering him because his young friend Percy Lubbock "thinks it complicated." Bosanquet observed that it was "an appeal for funds, though so well disguised I doubt if there will be much response!"

> Poor Mr. James went though the letter again, but found himself unable to take out a single word. "It's just exactly the plain facts as Richard Norton told them to me," he insisted. But plain facts translated into Jacobean terms! (25 November 1914)

No evidence of the paralyzing effect there, at least!

Perhaps the most substantial of Bosanquet's disagreements with the Master concerned two of Edith Wharton's novels. *Henry James at Work* refers us, half way through section VII, to James's preference for *The Reef* over the perennial favorite *Ethan Frome;* Bosanquet so fits that information into her interesting comments on James's annoyance with "inarticulate" human beings that she may seem to agree with that preference. The very opposite was true. James had dictated to her a letter of fulsome praise of *The Reef* for Edith Wharton, calling it "quite the finest thing you have done" and complimenting her as being "stronger and firmer and finer than all of them [George Eliot et al.] put together;

you go farther and say mieux" (4 and 9 December 1912, *Letters IV*, 644–46). A month later that praise was still rankling in Bosanquet's memory:

> It's such a good example, it seems to me, of his blind affection for an imitation of his own manner, for I don't really think Mrs. W. is so good in this rather tired book, with its overdone coincidences and its occasional false notes . . . as in the wonderful little masterpiece Ethan Frome. (Diary B, 13 January 1913)

It might be observed here that Theodora Bosanquet had by this time become, however modestly, a published author in her own right. In these years immediately preceding the Great War, a number of her items (essays, fiction, poems, and reviews) were appearing, especially in the *Saturday Westminster Gazette,* the same periodical that published Rupert Brooke's *Letters from America.* By January 1915 she had begun work on the epistolary novel in collaboration with Clara Smith; *Spectators* was published in London by Constable and Company in May 1916. J. B. Pinker, James's literary agent, had agreed to become the literary agent of Bosanquet in April 1913.

Her final estimate of Henry James as a great man and a consummate artist—fully justified, further, in his theory and practice of revision—by no means emerges from a mind overawed and paralyzed by the perceived stature of the Master. Although shy and inclined to be self-effacing, Bosanquet became increasingly independent-minded and self-reliant. Part of the value of *Henry James at Work* derives from her status as an objective and comparatively unbiased, if generally sympathetic, witness and reporter.

The extent of the responsible intimacy of Bosanquet's involvement with James's career is demonstrated by her activity during the final weeks of his life and her participation in the important posthumous tidying up of his professional affairs.[5] She took charge of domestic organization and financial obligations at 21 Carlyle Mansions (James's flat in Chelsea) immediately after his initial series of strokes in early December 1915, having informed the James family—especially William's widow (Alice) and eldest son (Harry)—in the United States

---

5. See Diary A, 2 December 1915 to 15 October 1916.

of his physical condition and then his progress, until they were able to reach England; she tended to necessary business correspondence and also kept James's close friends abreast of developments—Edith Wharton primarily, but also Jessie Allen, Rhoda Broughton, Lucy Clifford, Mrs. Charles Hunter, Percy Lubbock, and George and Fanny Prothero—thereby earning their respect, gratitude, and friendship. Bosanquet played a major role in the preparation of the Master's final publication of his lifetime for appearance in print. James had eagerly agreed to provide a preface for Rupert Brooke's *Letters from America;* proofs arrived in early December 1915, just after James had been incapacitated by his first strokes, so Bosanquet was obliged to undertake the proofreading. Furthermore, certain remarks in the text about Brooke's treatment at the hands of the *Westminster Gazette* (which had originally published the first thirteen of the letters) provoked the threat of a libel suit; at the request of Edward Marsh, Bosanquet satisfactorily revised the offending passage and facilitated publication in early 1916. She managed to reduce a page of typescript, about three-quarters of the way through the article, to a sentence of some forty words so that no seam shows and the stream of James's prose flows steadily on. And while relations between Mrs. William James and the willing Bosanquet were at that time strained, the doughty sister-in-law was able to praise the achievement of the amanuensis: "Henry would never know he hadn't written it himself."[6]

Bosanquet also typed up, at nephew Harry James's bidding, copies of many of his uncle's remaining manuscripts, such as the incomplete novel *The Ivory Tower* and book of memoirs *The Middle Years.* The question of producing an edition of James's letters involved Bosanquet as well, peripherally at first, but when it was decided (happily) that Percy Lubbock should take the task in hand (literary agent J. B. Pinker understandably preferred Edith Wharton), she was wisely invited to work with Lubbock on the project. Thus Bosanquet was there, intimately involved, until the end—and indeed well beyond. The two-volume edition of *The Letters of Henry James* was duly published in 1920.

II ✴. Well before that date, however, Theodora Bosanquet was gently launched in her own literary career; one of its principal currents, it

---

6. Marsh's letter of 11 December 1915 to Bosanquet actually downplays the threat of libel action: "Mr. Spender [counsel for the *Gazette*] will be seriously hurt at the

Theodora Bosanquet during
the Henry James years

Facsimile of Vanessa Bell's
original cover for
Henry James at Work, 1924

THE HOGARTH ESSAYS

HENRY JAMES AT WORK

THEODORA BOSANQUET

THE HOGARTH PRESS

Gertrude Mary Bosanquet and Theodora, ca. 1887, bMS Eng 1213.8.
By permission of the Houghton Library, Harvard University.

Theodora and parents, ca. 1887, bMS Eng 1213.8.
By permission of the Houghton Library, Harvard University.

Sketch of Dora Bosanquet by
Reginald H. Fox, April 1891,
bMS Eng 1213.8. By permission
of the Houghton Library, Harvard
University.

Theodora, age fifteen,
November 1895, bMS Eng 1213.8.
By permission of the Houghton
Library, Harvard University.

Theodora, ca. 1897, "a singularly unattractive specimen" in her hand,
bMS Eng 1213.8. By permission of the Houghton Library, Harvard University.

"Tennis, anyone?" Bosanquet at courtside, June 1901, bMS Eng 1213.8.
By permission of the Houghton Library, Harvard University.

Henry James on his seventieth birthday, 1913

Front entrance of Lamb House, West Street. The bow windows of the Garden Room used to extend into West Street at the spot where the tree now looks over the Garden wall.

Bosanquet's residence, at left with black trim, Mermaid Street, from October 1907.

now seems obvious, led her directly to *Henry James at Work*. The provenance of that publication may be said to begin with her discovery of James's fiction in the early 1890s and her serving as amanuensis from October 1907; but it can certainly be traced to her entering a contest in the *Saturday Westminster Review* for parodies of great authors. She submitted three parodies; that of Arnold Bennett won a handsome prize of three guineas, while that of Rose Macauley (whom Bosanquet admired enthusiastically) did not; the third, that of Henry James, earned special treatment. Naomi Royde Smith of the *Gazette's* editorial staff returned it to Bosanquet with a request that it be enlarged and the promise of early publication. In her diary Bosanquet gives this account of the item:

> I had great fun doing a parody of him for the Sat. Westminster competition the other day . . . a young attaché who has to do something or other, what doesn't matter, at Berlin in the presence of the Kaiser, the Grand Duke Nicholas, Joffre and the French and simply can't get them to meet. Final discovery that they share a single personality between then, a really Jacobean idea. (13 January 1915)

The claim that this idea is "really Jacobean" gains some clarification from the beginning of the paragraph in which the description occurs— a disparaging account of the Master's struggles with *The Sense of the Past,* "an essentially impossible idea, even 'psychically,'" she calls it. (This statement must not be mistaken as indicative of Bosanquet's dislike of psychic matters or even of her lack of interest in them. On the contrary, she was herself more than marginally involved in manifestations of psychic powers and phenomena, from palm-reading and tarot

---

imputation that he did not rate Brooke's contributions at their right value." He explains Brooke's misunderstanding of the *Gazette's* and James's erroneous idea of its mistreatment of the poet. Marsh accurately assesses the editorial task of removing the blemish, as he proposed it to Bosanquet: "Unfortunately the passage in the preface is deeply embedded in the context, & it is impossible to suggest a mere elision. . . . this would be mere botching. I am sure you will appreciate the dilemma, & I shd be very grateful to you if you cd suggest a way out." (Bosanquet Archive, Houghton Library, Harvard University.) When Marsh saw her achievement, "he approved" (Diary A, 18 December 1915). See Diary A, 9–18 December 1915.

cards to faith-healing and spiritualism. She attended meetings of the Society for Psychic Research, and her excitement on meeting William James was due not simply to his being another "great man," like his brother Henry, but principally to his important involvement in psychic research. Diary C gives a sampling of illustrative evidence of Bosanquet's interest and activity in that area.)

Then, within months of Henry James's death Bosanquet is busy at "the daily effort to lick an article on H.J. into shape" (Diary B, 17 July 1916). In early November she can report to her diary the response of Percy Lubbock and James's dear old friend Howard Sturgis to this critical endeavor: from the former, "a delightfully kind and encouraging letter, couldn't have been nicer," and from the latter a more reserved reaction with specific objections, "But otherwise he was too kind" (10 November 1916). On 5 December 1916 she delivers the typescript of her article to her agent, J. B. Pinker, and "Henry James" achieves publication in England in the *Fortnightly Review* for June 1917 and is immediately reprinted in August in the *Living Age* in England, and the *Bookman* in the United States. This essay offers a brief account of Bosanquet's acquaintance with James's fiction before her actual meeting with the Master. First, as "a girl of not more than twelve or thirteen years" she discovered in her father's study in their Devonshire farmhouse a copy of *The Europeans,* and second, "half a dozen years later" a friend lent her a copy of *The Two Magics*—"The Turn of the Screw" and "Covering End." Then the essay rehearses her first meeting with James and her employment as his amanuensis, and provides a fairly substantial anticipation of *Henry James at Work,* including a couple of pages on James's revision of his fiction for the New York Edition of his novels and tales, published between 1907 and 1909.

A more thorough canvassing of the topic of revision occurs in Bosanquet's "The Revised Version," published in the *Little Review* in August 1918, the number devoted to Henry James and including essays by T. S. Eliot and Ezra Pound. Eliot's essay "In Memory," reprinted from the *Egoist* for January 1918 (and there called "In Memory of Henry James"), may have exerted some influence on Bosanquet's next published essay on James, "The Record of Henry James," in the *Yale Review* for October 1920, which was obviously prompted by the publication of Lubbock's edition of *The Letters of Henry James.*

"The Record of Henry James" contributed substantially to sections

IV, V, and IX of *Henry James at Work;* its contribution to sections VII and VIII overlaps appreciably that of the 1917 "Henry James." There are two points, however, that are of particular significance in Bosanquet's appraisal here of James the artist. The first is possibly derived from the Eliot essay just mentioned: "In Memory" contains the now familiar—and often maliciously appropriated, without context—comment on James, "He had a mind so fine that no idea could violate it." Bosanquet's development of that perception may strike some alert readers as more easily apprehendable and offering a clearer illumination than Eliot's own. We can consider that development more carefully in a moment.

The second point is a much fuller expression of the phenomenon of James's commitment to his art—to his muse, specifically—than Bosanquet had room for in the opening lines of section VII of *Henry James at Work,* where she observes that "Henry James . . . lived a life consecrated to the service of a jealous, insatiable, and supremely rewarding goddess, and all his activities had essential reference to that service." In "The Record of Henry James" she gives liberal accommodation to the subject.

> He was possessed by a conviction as clear and abiding as the belief of any cloistered saint, that the power which worked through him would sustain and inspire him to the end. Even in his young days the sense of almost miraculous support is evident, but it increases in strength with the passage of years. . . . He was always serenely conscious that he was the instrument of a divinity punctually responsive to his ardent and repeated pressure of the spring of inspiration.[7]

She then refers the reader to Lubbock's introduction to *The Letters of Henry James,* where he quotes passages from James's notebooks that graphically illuminate her observations on James and his muse: she calls this his "fullest expression" of his faith. Lubbock's long quotation (pp. xx–xxi of the Introduction) is an amalgam of three sections of James's notes for "The K.B. Case and Mrs. Max"; the most lyrical and moving lines are doubtless these:

---

7. "Record of Henry James," 147–48.

I simply make an appeal to all the powers and forces and divinities to whom I've ever been loyal and who haven't failed me yet—after all; never, never yet! . . . Causons causons, mon bon . . . my poor blest old Genius pats me so admirably and lovingly on the back that I turn, I screw round, and bend my lips to passionately, in my gratitude, kiss its hands.[8]

It is highly unlikely that Virginia and Leonard Woolf could have been entirely ignorant of Theodora Bosanquet's writings on James between 1917 and 1920; it is nonetheless probable that Bosanquet sent those essays unsolicited to the proprietors of the Hogarth Press in Tavistock Square. A hint that Mrs. Woolf had at least glimpsed "The Revised Version"—as it rubbed elbows with essays by Eliot and Pound in the American magazine the *Little Review*—lurks in her first reference to Bosanquet. Virginia Woolf's letter of 1 December 1923 to Gerald Brennan notes that she "ought to be reading 4 manuscripts for the Hogarth Press . . . a third by an astute and bold American [*sic*] who was Henry James's secretary."[9] She was still chastising herself in a diary entry on 23 February 1924 for not getting to the manuscript of "Miss Bosanquet on Henry James."[10] That reminder obviously did the trick, for she wrote to Bosanquet on the very next day:

I have read your article with great interest. You are right in thinking that the article I had heard of was about Henry James's methods of work, dictation and so on. But we think your idea of combining the different articles a very good one. Would it be possible to begin by giving your personal memories, which would be of the highest value as there is no account I think of his methods during his late period. . . . About 10,000 words would be as much as are able manage. We should issue it as a pamphlet,

---

8. "The K.B. Case and Mrs. Max" is a preliminary note for James's unfinished novel *The Ivory Tower;* see *The Complete Notebooks of Henry James,* ed. Leon Edel and Lyall H. Powers (New York: Oxford University Press, 1987), 260–61, 268. See especially Edel's introduction to that volume, "Colloquies with his Good Angel," xiii–xiv.
9. *The Letters of Virginia Woolf,* vol. 3, *A Change of Perspective, 1923–1928,* ed. Nigel Nicolson (London: Hogarth Press, 1977), 78.
10. *The Diary of Virginia Woolf,* vol. 2, *1920–1924,* ed. Anna Olivier Bell (London: Hogarth Press, 1978), 292.

and would give you 25% of the profits. I think it should make a most interesting little book.[11]

Henry James at Work was in Virginia Woolf's hands by 7 November 1924, when she wrote Bosanquet a very complimentary letter calling the essay "a great success" and adding, "you have got an immense deal into it, and made it come together perfectly as a whole."[12] It was published that month as one of the first in the series of Hogarth Essays.

The Woolfs conceived of the series—against all odds—early in that year. Leonard described the project to Harold Nicolson in a letter of 6 July 1924 as one "foredoomed to failure because every publisher knows that the pamphlet is unsaleable. However," he continued bravely, expressing their optimism, "we are going to attempt it and we are beginning with pamphlets by Roger Fry, my wife, and a Miss Bosanquet on Henry James."[13] *Henry James at Work* is number 3 in the series.

Another venture of the Hogarth Press was the production, beginning in 1917, of handprinted books. *Henry James at Work* is the only one of the Hogarth Essays to have been handprinted—a delightful "fluke"—and it boasted a cover design by Vanessa Bell.[14]

A second edition of *Henry James at Work* was published by the Hogarth Press in 1927. There are no changes of great consequence in the new edition; the most substantial modification is found in her description of James's appearance. In the first edition, "He might perhaps have been some species of disguised cardinal, or even a Roman nobleman"; the second alters that to "an eminent cardinal in mufti, or even a Roman senator." In 1928, Doubleday, Doran in New York published *The Hogarth Essays,* a selection of eleven of the pamphlets published by the Hogarth Press; the ninth is a reprint of the first edition of *Henry James at Work.*

---

11. Woolf, *Letters,* 3:89.

12. *The Letters of the Virginia Woolf,* vol. 6, *Leave the Letters Till We're Dead, 1936–1941,* ed. Nigel Nicolson (London: Hogarth Press, 1980), 506.

13. *Letters of Leonard Woolf,* ed. Francis Spottis (New York: Harcourt Brace Jovanovich, 1989), 264.

14. So called by Donna E. Rhein, *The Handprinted Books of Leonard and Virginia Woolf at the Hogarth Press, 1917–1932* (Ann Arbor, Mich.: UMI Research Press, 1985), 13. See photo section, p. 1.

III 🐜. Perhaps the most original contribution of this pamphlet to the critical appreciation of Henry James's writings resides in the series of
observations that constitute the bulk of sections V through IX, which
may be divided according to these themes: (1) revision, V; (2) drama,
VI; (3) commitment to art, VII; (4) ideas, VIII; and (5) "international," IX. These may appear to be a congeries of fairly discrete topics; considered in terms of their interrelationships, however, they can
be seen to coalesce into a strongly unified commentary on James's art
of fiction.

Theodora Bosanquet's adaptation and sharp focusing of James's
defense of his revisions emphasize the enrichment and revitalization he
achieved by that practice: "the revised version," she insists in V, "is
nearly always richer and more alive." As her essay continues, it
becomes evident that her concern is with the increased lifelikeness he
produced by his revisions; and that realistic quality depends on a number of features that the essay touches on in its latter half. The effect of
her demonstration is cumulative. A note in her diary for 22 October
1915 helps us grasp the initial step in that process. Of H. G. Wells's
The Research Magnificent Bosanquet remarks, "It's interesting and valuable to have all these human documents and these flashes and impressions of life as it seems to H. G. Wells—but that makes one long only
the more eagerly for the equally vivid and sincere impressions of life as
it shows itself to other people."[15] It is not simply facts we need, that
note clearly implies, not just the "human documents" that reproduce
"the look of things," but an arrangement and presentation that render
"the look that conveys their meaning" (as James made the distinction
in his "The Art of Fiction," 1884). Bosanquet's phrase "vivid and sincere" in the diary further qualifies her "richer and more alive" in the
Hogarth essay: careful representation makes the fiction more lifelike,
self-contained, able to stand on its own feet, and apparently free of the
author's controlling hand.

The concern of section VI of *Henry James at Work* adds impetus to the
cumulative effect of the argument. It rehearses James's second venture
into the theater, but it quickly leads to the relationship between drama
and fiction as it specifies the transgeneric adaptations—fiction into play

---

15. See Diary B.

and vice versa—that characterized that period of James's career. Discussion of that relationship recalls certain relevant observations made in section III that had already established the connection of Jamesian fiction and drama. Bosanquet there reminded us that James "tended to dramatize all the material that life gave him" and that he "prefigured his novels as staged performances, arranged in acts and scenes." The next paragraph there carries us an important step further. Bosanquet makes the point that James's "breaking ground," his preliminary ruminations about his characters and their actions, resulted in a typescript that was virtually never consulted thereafter; it had served its purpose: "The knowledge of all the conscious motives and concealments of his creatures, gained by unwearied observation of their attitudes behind the scenes, enabled Henry James to exhibit them with a final confidence that dispensed with explanations." The key word there is "exhibit." The point about his being enabled to dispense with explanations refers us again to the importance of creating fiction that comes to the reader immediately and without the explanatory touch that would blatantly manipulate the innocent reader. Bosanquet concludes her paragraph with this simple truth: "between the people created by Henry James lying is as frequent as among mortals and not any easier to detect." *That* is dramatic rendering.

If James's fiction is so deceptively realistic, so emphatically like the experience of actual life, readers must be as attentive to the material before them as sensible citizens must be to the world that confronts them. While section VII quite appropriately emphasizes James's service to his demanding and rewarding muse, it also leads directly to this necessary conclusion: "It was his theory that if readers don't keep up with him—as they admittedly didn't always—the fault was entirely in their failure of attention." Truly artistic realism does make its demands on the attention.

The concluding two sections of *Henry James at Work* are challenging in their presentation of guidelines. Section VIII develops an observation that may have received impetus from T. S. Eliot's comment that James "had a mind so fine that no idea could violate it." And *violate* is the crucial term. After alerting us to the fact that James's letters do not serve as explanations of his fiction, Bosanquet indicates their signal revelation about the importance of impressions to James and of his being "unusually impervious to everything which is not an impression of visual images or a sense of a human situation." She thus arrives at the principal issue:

> He was very little troubled by a number of ideas which press with an increasing weight upon the minds of most educated persons . . . he never reckoned it to be any part of his business to sit in judgment on the deeds of men working in alien material for inartistic ends, or to speculate about the nature of the universe or the conflict or reconciliation of science with religion.

A blunter and more direct version of the issue in the diary entry of 1 August 1916 offers reinforcement as it chastises Rebecca West for slighting the Master's "greatness": "He went so much further than anyone else has ever been along his own line just *because* he spent all his time at the one business of receiving and analysing and appraising and transmitting the impressions life showered on him. It's ridiculous to blame him for not appreciating the lessons of history and the rights of women." Bosanquet is trying to establish an important distinction between *life* and *ideas about life*. The passage that draws this section to a close with its words on "cabinets and parties and politics" on the one hand, and "the customs of a country" on the other, intends to illustrate the distinction in question. The purpose is evidently to reiterate from an adjacent point of view the necessity of sustaining the dramatic quality of fiction: its business is to "exhibit" life without deviation into the explanatory or discursive or, least of all, the argumentative and polemical modes. This is, after all, very like the attitude Virginia Woolf presented in the papers she read to the women of Newnham and Girton Colleges in October 1928, that the mind of an artist must be "incandescent"—like Shakespeare's mind:

> All desire to protest, to preach, to proclaim an injury, to pay off a score, to make the world a witness of some hardship or grievance was fired out of him and consumed. Therefore his poetry flows from him free and unimpeded. If ever a human being got his work expressed completely, it was Shakespeare.[16]

16. *A Room of One's Own* (New York: Harcourt Brace, 1929), 99.

The final section of *Henry James at Work* discusses the topic of James's nationality, whether the expatriate from the United States became British, whether his best work was international in its concerns as in its aspect. The conclusion reached adds the last touch to Bosanquet's tacit definition of Jamesian literary realism. Just as it was not *ideas about* but *impressions of* common human behavior and interaction that occupied his artistic mind, so it was not, finally, the superficies of national identity that held his artistic interest. Bosanquet's decision that James "was never really English or American or even Cosmopolitan" is persuasive. Her consequent observation completes her conception of Henry James man and artist: "To-day, with the complete record before us . . . we can understand how little those international relations that engaged Henry James's attention mattered to his genius." This conception is fleshed out in the paragraph that begins, "We may conclude that the nationalities of his betrayed and triumphant victims are not an important factor," and ends with "a reiterated and passionate plea for the fullest freedom of development, unimperilled by reckless and barbarous stupidity."

Bosanquet would have us recognize that James's novels and tales are *fiction,* what R. P. Blackmur liked to call "a theoretic form of life"; that James strove to give his fiction as convincing an appearance of life as he could—to make a story self-supporting, self-expressive, and free of a controlling author's manipulative and betraying hand, and thus as immediate as a play upon the stage or as life itself; that a piece of fiction is a kind of elaborate metaphor that offers serious entertainment. She thus urges recognition that the artistic character of James's fiction and its profoundly moral concern mesh and accommodate each other reciprocally to demonstrate what human behavior is life-enhancing and what life-diminishing. She observes that James "knew that nothing in life mattered compared with spiritual decency," and thus signals the essence of James's *Comédie humaine.*

Theodora Bosanquet was a pioneer critic-biographer in the study of Henry James and gave early impetus to appreciation of his artistic achievement that was predominant for over half a century. Her contribution has been rather overlooked. Leon Edel described her at the moment of entering the Master's service as a "slim young woman . . . rather boyish"; and on the day of her arrival James described her in a letter to Fanny Prothero as the "robust Miss Bosanquet." Had she been more distinctly "boyish" and more assertively "robust," she might have enjoyed in those prejudiced years a more intelligent and honest recognition. Now that the Jamesian field is fuller of boyish, robust, assertive, and gentle Jamesiennes, Bosanquet should receive a broader welcome. Perhaps republication of her essay on James will earn the attention and respect she deserves.

In view of her enlightened championing of Henry James's defense of revision, and of an author's right to retouch and improve, I have selected Theodora Bosanquet's second edition of *Henry James at Work* for republication here.

Henry James at Work

By Theodora Bosanquet

I 🐝 I knew nothing of Henry James beyond the revelation of his novels and tales before the summer of 1907. Then, as I sat in a top-floor office near Whitehall one August morning, compiling a very full index to the *Report of the Royal Commission on Coast Erosion,* my ears were struck by the astonishing sound of passages from *The Ambassadors* being dictated to a young typist. Neglecting my Blue-book, I turned round to watch the operator ticking off sentences which seemed to be at least as much of a surprise to her as they were to me. When my bewilderment had broken into a question, I learnt that Henry James was on the point of coming back from Italy,[1] that he had asked to be provided with an amanuensis, and that the lady at the typewriter was making acquaintance with his style. Without any hopeful design on supplanting her, I lodged an immediate petition that I might be allowed the next opportunity of filling the post, supposing she should ever abandon it. The established candidate was not enthusiastic about the prospect before her, was even genuinely relieved to look in another direction. If I set about practicing typewriting on a Remington machine at once, I could be interviewed by Henry James as soon as he arrived in London. Within an hour I had begun work on the typewriter. By the time he was ready to interview me, I could tap out paragraphs of *The Ambassadors* at quite a fair speed.

He asked no questions at that interview about my speed on a typewriter or about anything else. The friend to whom he had applied for an amanuensis had told him that I was sufficiently the right young

---

1. James had spent some four months on the continent from early March, including seven weeks in Italy; he was back in Lamb House on 7 July.

woman for his purpose and he had relied on her word. He had, at the
best, little hope of any young woman beyond docility. We sat in arm-
chairs on either side of a fireless grate while we observed each other. I
suppose he found me harmless and I know that I found him amazing.
He was much more massive than I had expected, much broader and
stouter and stronger.[2] I remembered that someone had told me he
used to be taken for a sea-captain when he wore a beard, but it was
clear that now, with the beard shaved away, he would hardly have
passed for, say, an admiral, in spite of the keen grey eyes set in a face
burned to a colourable sea-faring brown by the Italian sun. No successful naval officer could have afforded to keep that sensitive mobile
mouth. After the interview I wondered what kind of impression one
might have gained from a chance encounter in some such observation
cell as a railway carriage. Would it have been possible to fit him
confidently into any single category? He had reacted with so much success against both the American accent and the English manner that he
seemed only doubtfully Anglo-Saxon. He might perhaps have been an
eminent cardinal in mufti, or even a Roman senator amusing himself
by playing the part of a Sussex squire. The observer could at least have
guessed that any part he chose to assume would be finely conceived
and generously played, for his features were all cast in the classical
mould of greatness. He might very well have been a merciful Caesar
or a benevolent Napoleon, and a painter[3] who worked at his portrait a
year or two later was excusably reminded of so many illustrious mak-
ers of history that he declared it would be a hard task to isolate the
individual character in the model.

If the interview was overwhelming, it had none of the usual awk-
wardness of such curious conversations. Instead of critical angles and
disconcerting silences, there were only benign curves and ample reas-
surances. There was an encouraging gaiety in an expanse of bright
check waistcoat. He invited me to ask any questions I liked, but I had
none to ask. I wanted nothing but to be allowed to go to Rye and work
his typewriter. He was prepared, however, with his statements and,
once I was seated opposite him, the strong, slow stream of his delib-

2. Bosanquet recorded her first impression of James in her diary, 22 August 1907;
see Diary A under that date.
3. Jacques-Emile Blanche (1861–1942), French popular portraitist and writer.

erate speech played over me without ceasing. He had it on his mind to tell me the conditions of life and labour at Rye, and he unburdened himself fully, with numberless amplifications and qualifications but without any real break. It would be a dull business, he warned me, and I should probably find Rye a dull place. He told me of rooms in Mermaid Street, "very simple; rustic and antique—but that is the case for everything near my house, and this particular little old house is very near mine, and I know the good woman for kind and worthy and a convenient cook and in short—." It was settled at once that I should take the rooms,[4] and that I should begin my duties in October.

II 🐎. Since winter was approaching, Henry James had begun to use a paneled, green-painted room on the upper floor of Lamb House for his work. It was known simply as the green room. It had many advantages as a winter workroom, for it was small enough to be easily warmed and a wide south window caught all the morning sunshine. The window overhung the smooth, green lawn, shaded in summer by a mulberry tree, surrounded by roses and enclosed behind a tall, brick wall. It never failed to give the owner pleasure to look out of this convenient window at his English garden where he could watch his English gardener[5] digging the flower-beds or mowing the lawn or sweeping up fallen leaves. There was another window for the afternoon sun, looking towards Winchelsea and doubly glazed against the force of the westerly gales. Three high bookcases, two big writing-desks and an easy chair filled most of the space in the green room, but left enough clear floor for the restricted amount of the pacing exercise that was indispensable to literary composition. On summer days Henry James liked better to work in the large "garden room"[6] which gave him a longer stretch for perambulation and a window overlooking the cobbled street that curved up the hill past his door. He liked to be able to relieve the tension of a difficult sentence by a glance down

---

4. Her rooms were in Marigold Cottage; her landlady, Mrs. Holland.

5. George Gammon.

6. The Garden Room was a small structure, separate from Lamb House proper and with a separate heating system which it shared with the adjacent greenhouse. Bosanquet regularly found that the first few weeks of spring there were rather stifling. The Garden Room was destroyed by enemy bombs on 18 August 1940. See photo section, p. 8.

the street; he enjoyed hailing a passing friend or watching a motor-car pant up the sharp little slope. The sight of one of these vehicles could be counted on to draw from him a vigorous outburst of amazement, admiration, or horror for the complications of an age that produced such efficient monsters for gobbling protective distance.

The business of acting as a medium between the spoken and the typewritten word was at first as alarming as it was fascinating. The most handsome and expensive typewriters exercise as vicious an influence as any others over the spelling of the operator, and the new pattern of a Remington machine which I found installed offered a few additional problems. But Henry James's patience during my struggles with that baffling machine was unfailing—he watched me helplessly, for he was one of the few men without the smallest pretension to the understanding of a machine—and he was as easy to spell from as an open dictionary. The experience of years had evidently taught him that it was not safe to leave any word or more than one syllable to luck. He took pains to pronounce every pronounceable letter, he always spelt out words which the ear might confuse with others, and he never left a single punctuation mark unuttered, except sometimes that necessary point, the full stop. Occasionally, in a low "aside," he would interject a few words for the enlightenment of the amanuensis, adding, for instance, after the spelling out of The Newcomes, that the words were the title of a novel by one Thackeray.[7]

The practice of dictation was begun in the 'nineties.[8] By 1907 it was a confirmed habit, its effects being easily recognizable in his style, which became more and more like free, involved, unanswered talk. "I know," he once said to me, "that I'm too diffuse when I'm dictating." But he found dictation not only an easier but a more inspiring method of composing than writing with his own hand, and he considered that the gain in expression more than compensated for any loss of concision. The spelling out of the words, the indication of commas, were scarcely felt as a drag on the movement of his thought. "It all seems," he once explained, "to be so much more effectively and unceasingly pulled out of me in speech than in writing." Indeed, at the time when I

7. William Makepeace Thackeray (1811–63), English novelist; The Newcomes (1853–55).
8. James's practice of dictation actually began in February 1897, after severe and recurrent pain in his right wrist—"writer's cramp"—obliged him to hire a typist.

began to work for him, he had reached a stage at which the click of a Remington machine acted as a positive spur. He found it more difficult to compose to the music of any other make. During the fortnight when the Remington was out of order he dictated to an Oliver typewriter with evident discomfort, and he found it almost impossibly disconcerting to speak to something that made no responsive sound at all. Once or twice when he was ill and in bed I took down a note or two by hand, but as a rule he liked to have a typewriter moved into his bedroom for even the shortest letters. Yet there were to the end certain kinds of work which he was obliged to do with a pen. Plays, if they were to be kept within the limits of possible performance, and short stories, if they were to remain within the bounds of publication in a monthly magazine, must be written by hand. He was well aware that the manual labour of writing was his best aid to desired brevity. The plays—such a play as *The Outcry,*[9] for instance—were copied straight from his manuscript, since he was too much afraid of "the murderous limits of the English theatre" to risk the temptation of dictation and embroidery. With the short stories he allowed himself a little more freedom, dictating them from his written draft and expanding them as he went to an extent which inevitably defeated his original purpose. It was almost literally true to say of the sheaf of tales collected in *The Finer Grain*[10] that they were all written in response to a simple request for a short story for *Harper's Monthly Magazine*. The length was to be about 5,000 words and each promising idea was cultivated in the optimistic belief that it would produce a flower too frail and small to demand any exhaustive treatment. But even under the pressure of being written by hand, with dictated interpolations rigidly restricted, each in turn pushed out to lengths that no chopping could reduce to the word limit. The tale eventually printed was *Crapy Cornelia,* but, although it was the shortest of the batch, it was thought too long to be published in one number and appeared in two sections, to the great annoyance of the author.

---

9. Prepared in 1909–10 for Charles Frohman's repertory program in London, the play never reached the stage because of the combined influence of James's illness and the death of King Edward VII. He converted it into a successful novel (London: Methuen; and New York: Scribner's, 1911), under the same title.

10. New York: Scribner's; and London: Methuen, 1910.

III 🐎 The method adopted for full-length novels was very different. With a clear run of 100,000 words or more before him, Henry James always cherished the delusive expectation of being able to fit his theme quite easily between the covers of a volume. It was not until he was more than half way through that the problem of space began to be embarrassing. At the beginning he had no questions of compression to attend to, and he "broke ground," as he said, by talking to himself day by day about the characters and construction until the persons and their actions were vividly present to his inward eye. This soliloquy was of course recorded on the typewriter. He had from far back tended to dramatise all the material that life gave him, and he more and more prefigured his novels as staged performances, arranged in acts and scenes, with the characters making their observed entrances and exits. These scenes he worked out until he felt himself so thoroughly possessed of the action that he could begin dictation of the book itself—a process which has been incorrectly described by one critic as re-dictation from a rough draft. It was nothing of the kind. Owners of the volumes containing *The Ivory Tower* or *The Sense of the Past*[11] have only to turn to the Notes printed at the end to see that the scenario dictated in advance contains practically none of the phrases used in the final work. The two sets of notes are a different and a much more interesting literary record than a mere draft. They are the framework set up for imagination to clothe with the spun web of life. But they are not bare framework. They are elaborate and abundant. They are the kind of exercise described in *The Death of the Lion* as "a great gossiping eloquent letter—the overflow into talk of an artist's amorous design."[12] But the design was thus mapped out with a clear understanding that at a later stage and at closer quarters the subject might grow away from the plan. "In the intimacy of composition pre-noted proportions and arrangements do most uncommonly insist on

11. These two novels of James's, left unfinished at his death, were published in 1917 with prefaces by Percy Lubbock (London: Collins; and New York: Scribner's); a small number of copies of the Scribner edition were bound uniformly with the New York Edition as volumes 25 and 26 of an enlarged edition.

12. The short story was serialized in *The Yellow Book,* April 1894, and published in *Terminations* (London: Heinemann; and New York: Harper's, 1895); included in vol. 15 of the New York Edition. The quotation, from the last sentence of section III, actually ends with "amorous plan."

making themselves different by shifts and variations, always improving, which impose themselves as one goes and keep the door open always to something *more* right and *more* related. It is subject to that constant possibility, all the while, that one does pre-note and tentatively sketch."

The preliminary sketch was seldom consulted after the novel began to take permanent shape, but the same method of "talking out" was resorted to at difficult points of the narrative as it progressed, always for the sake of testing in advance the values of the persons involved in a given situation, so that their creator should ensure their right action both for the development of the drama and the truth of their relations to each other. The knowledge of all the conscious motives and concealments of his creatures, gained by unwearied observation of their attitudes behind the scenes, enabled Henry James to exhibit them with a final confidence that dispensed with explanations. Among certain stumbling blocks in the path of the perfect comprehension of his readers is their uneasy doubt of the sincerity of the conversational encounters recorded. Most novelists provide some clue to help their readers to distinguish truth from falsehood, and in the theatre, although husbands and wives may be deceived by lies, the audience is usually privy to the plot. But a study of the Notes to *The Ivory Tower* will make it clear that between people created by Henry James lying is as frequent as among mortals and not any easier to detect.

For the volumes of memories, *A Small Boy and Others, Notes of a Son and Brother,* and the uncompleted *Middle Years,*[13] no preliminary work was needed. A straight dive into the past brought to the surface treasure after treasure, a wealth of material which became embarrassing. The earlier book was begun in 1911, after Henry James had returned from a year in the United States, where he had been called by his brother's fatal illness.[14] He had come back, after many seasons in coun-

---

13. The first two were published in 1913 and 1914, respectively, by Scribner in New York and Macmillan in London; the third, left unfinished, was serialized in *Scribner's Magazine* October–November 1917, and published as a whole in London by Collins and in New York by Scribner's in 1917.

14. William James and his wife were in Europe seeking a cure for William's failing health. James accompanied his severely ailing brother and his wife back to the United States in August 1910; William died at Chocorua shortly thereafter. James returned to Lamb House on 9 August 1911.

try solitude, to his former love of the friendly London winter, and for the first few months after his return from America he lodged near the Reform Club and came to the old house in Chelsea where I was living and where he had taken a room for his work. It was a quiet room, long and narrow and rather dark—he used to speak of it as "my Chelsea cellar."[15] There he settled down to write what, as he outlined it to me, was to be a set of notes to his brother William's early letters, prefaced by a brief account of the family into which they were both born. But an entire volume of memories was finished before bringing William to an age for writing letters, and *A Small Boy* came to a rather abrupt end as a result of the writer's sudden decision that a break must be made at once if the flood of remembrance was not to drown his pious intention.

It was extraordinarily easy for him to recover the past; he had always been sensitive to impressions and his mind was stored with records of exposure. All he had to do was to render his sense of those records as adequately as he could. Each morning, after reading over the pages written the day before, he would settle down in a chair for an hour or so of conscious effort. Then, lifted on a rising tide of inspiration, he would get up and pace up and down the room, sounding out the periods in tones of resonant assurance. At such times he was beyond reach of irrelevant sounds or sights. Hosts of cats—a tribe he usually routed with shouts of execration—might wail outside the window, phalanxes of motor-cars bearing dreaded visitors might hoot at the door. He heard nothing of them. The only thing that could arrest his progress was the escape of a word he wanted to use. When that had vanished he broke off the rhythmic pacing and made his way to a chimney-piece or book-case tall enough to support his elbows while he rested his head in his hands and audibly pursued the fugitive.

IV 🐾 In the autumn of 1907, when I began to tap the Remington typewriter at Henry James's dictation, he was engaged in the arduous task

---

15. She could not come to James's rooms in the Reform Club to take dictation. At Christmas 1909 he had inquired about a room in King's Cross Mansions, where Bosanquet and Nellie Bradley had just taken a little flat. He appealed more urgently in the fall of 1911 for "a seat and temple for the Remington and the priestess" (27 October). She found him a pair of rooms—with private entrance, fireplace, and bath—adjoining her flat at 10 Lawrence St. in Chelsea, near 21 Carlyle Mansions, where he found a flat on his own and moved in at the beginning of 1913.

of preparing his Novels and Tales for the definitive New York edition, published in 1909. Since it was only between breakfast and luncheon that he undertook what he called "inventive" work, he gave the hours from half-past ten to half-past one to the composition of the prefaces which are so interesting a feature of the edition. In the evenings, he read over again the work of former years, treating the printed pages like so many proof-sheets of extremely corrupt text. The revision was a task he had seen in advance as formidable. He had cultivated the habit of forgetting past achievements almost to the pitch of a sincere conviction that nothing he had written before 1890 could come with any shred of credit through the ordeal of critical inspection. On a morning when he was obliged to give time to the selection of a set of tales for a forthcoming volume, he confessed that the difficulty of the selection was mainly the difficulty of reading them all. "They seem," he said, "so bad until I *have* read them that I can't force myself to go through them except with a pen in my hand, altering as I go the crudities and ineptitudes that to my sense deform each page."[16] Unfamiliarity and adverse prejudice are rare advantages for a writer to bring to the task of choosing among his own works. For Henry James the prejudice might give way to half reluctant appreciation as the unfamiliarity passed into recognition, but it must be clear to every reader of the prefaces that he never lost the sense of being paternally responsible for two distinct families.[17] For the earlier brood, acknowledged fruit of his alliance with Romance, he claimed indulgence on the ground of their youthful spontaneity, their confident assurance, their rather touching good faith. One catches echoes of a plea that these elderly youngsters may not be too closely compared, to their inevitable disadvantage, with the richly endowed, the carefully bred, the highly civilised and sensitised children of his second marriage, contracted with that wealthy bride, Experience. Attentive readers of the novels may perhaps find the distinction between these two groups less remarkable than it seemed to their writer. They may even wonder whether the second marriage was not rather a silver wedding, with the old romantic mistress cleverly disguised as a woman of the world. The

---

16. These words were evidently *spoken* to Bosanquet.

17. Paragraphs 9 and 10 of the preface to *The Golden Bowl* develop the family metaphor in reference to his early work to be revised, as do other of his prefaces.

different note was possibly due more to the substitution of dictation for pen and ink than to any profound change of heart. But whatever the reason, their author certainly found it necessary to spend a good deal of time working on the earlier tales before he considered them fit for appearance in the company of those composed later. Some members of the elder family he entirely cast off, not counting them worth the expense of completely new clothes. Others he left in place more from a necessary, though deprecated, respect for the declared taste of the reading public than because he loved them for their own sake. It would, for instance, have been difficult to exclude *Daisy Miller*[18] from any representative collection of his work, yet the popularity of the tale had become almost a grievance. To be acclaimed as the author of *Daisy Miller* by persons blandly unconscious of *The Wings of the Dove* or *The Golden Bowl*[19] was a reason among many for Henry James's despair of intelligent comprehension. Confronted repeatedly with *Daisy,* he felt himself rather in the position of some *grande dame* who, with a jewel-case of sparkling diamonds, is constrained by her admirers always to appear in the simple string of moonstones worn at her first dance.

From the moment he began to read over the earlier tales, he found himself involved in the highly practical examination of the scope and limits of permissible revision. Poets, as he pointed out, have often revised their verse with good effect.[20] Why should the novelist not have equal license? The only sound reason for not altering anything is a conviction that it cannot be improved. It was Henry James's profound conviction that he could improve his early writing in nearly every sentence. Not to revise would have been to confess to a loss of faith in himself, and it was not likely that the writer who had fasted for forty years in the wilderness of British and American misconceptions without yielding a scrap of intellectual integrity to editorial or publishing tempters should have lost faith in himself. But he was well aware that the game of revision must be played with a due observance of the rules. He held that no novelist can safely afford to repudiate a

18. Serialized in the *Cornhill Magazine,* June and July 1878; published in New York by Harper, 1878; included in vol. 18 of the New York Edition.

19. *Wings of the Dove* (New York: Scribner; and London: Constable, 1902); vols. 19–20 of the New York Edition; *The Golden Bowl* (New York: Scribner; and London: Methuen, 1904); vols. 23–24 of the New York Edition.

20. Preface to *The Golden Bowl,* paragraphs 11 and 12.

fundamental understanding with his readers that the tale he has to tell
is at least as true as history and the figures he has set in motion at least
as independently alive as the people we see in offices and motor-cars.
He allowed himself few freedoms with any recorded appearances or
actions, although occasionally the temptation to correct a false gesture, to make it "right," was too strong to be resisted. We have a
pleasant instance of this correction in the second version of *The American.*[21] At her first appearance, the old Marquise de Bellegarde had
acknowledged the introduction of Newman by returning his handshake "with a sort of British positiveness which reminded him that she
was the daughter of the Earl of St. Dunstan's." In the later edition she
behaves differently. "Newman came sufficiently near to the old lady by
the fire to take in that she would offer him no handshake. . . . Madame
de Bellegarde looked hard at him and refused what she did refuse with
a sort of a British positiveness which reminded him that she was the
daughter of the Earl of St. Dunstan's." There were good reasons why
the Marquise should have denied Newman a welcoming handshake.
Her attitude throughout the book was to be consistently hostile and
should never have been compromised by the significantly British grip.
Yet it is almost shocking to see her snatching back her first card after
playing it for so many years. She was to perform less credible actions
than shaking hands with an innocent American as her progenitor knew
very well. He invited his readers, in the preface to *The American*[22] to
observe the impossible behavior of the noble Bellegarde family, but he
realized that since they had been begotten in absurdity the Bellegardes
could under no stress of revision achieve a very solid humanity. The
best he could do for them was to let a faint consciousness flush the
mind of Valentin, the only detached member of the family. In the first
edition Valentin warned his friend of the Bellegarde peculiarities with
the easy good faith of the younger Henry James under the spell of the
magic word "Europe." "My mother is strange, my brother is strange,
and I verily believe I am stranger than either. Old trees have queer
cracks, old races have odd secrets." To this statement he added in the

---

21. Serialized in *Atlantic Monthly,* June 1876 to May 1877; published in Boston by
Osgood and in London by Ward, Lock & Co., 1877; vol. 2 of the New York Edition.
22. See fourth- and third-last paragraphs of preface.

revised version: "We're fit for a museum or a Balzac novel." A comparable growth of ironic perception was allowed to Roderick Hudson,[23] whose comment on Rowland's admission of his heroically silent passion for Mary Garland, "It's like something in a novel," was altered to: "It's like something in a bad novel."

V 🐿 But the legitimate business of revision was, for Henry James, neither substitution nor re-arrangement. It was the demonstration of values implicit in the earlier work, the retrieval of neglected opportunities for adequate "renderings." "It was," as he explained in his final preface, "all sensibly, as if the clear matter being still there, even as a shining expanse of snow spread over a plain, my exploring tread, for application to it, had quite unlearned the old pace and found itself naturally falling into another, which might sometimes more or less agree with the original tracks, but might most often, or very nearly, break the surface in other places. What was thus predominantly interesting to note, at all events, was the high spontaneity of these deviations and differences, which became thus things not of choice but of immediate and perfect necessity: necessity to the end of dealing with the quantities in question at all."[24] On every page the act of re-reading became automatically one with the act of re-writing, and the revised parts are just "those rigid conditions of re-perusal, registered; so many close notes, as who should say, on the particular vision of the matter itself that experience had at last made the only possible one." These are words written with the clear confidence of the artist, who in complete possession of his "faculties," has no need to bother himself with doubts as to his ability to write better at the end of a lifetime of hard work and varied experience than at the beginning. He knew he could write better. His readers have not always agreed with his own view. They have denounced the multiplication of qualifying clauses, the imposition of a system of punctuation which, although rigid and orderly, occasionally fails to act as a guide to immediate comprehension of the writer's

23. *Roderick Hudson,* serialized in *Atlantic Monthly,* January–December 1875, published in Boston by Osgood and in London by Macmillan, 1879; vol. 1 of the New York Edition.

24. Preface to *The Golden Bowl,* last two sentences of paragraph 8; first sentence ends "in other places."

intention, and the increasing passion for adverbial interpositions. "Adjectives are the sugar of literature and adverbs the salt," was Henry James's reply to a criticism which once came to his ears.

It must be admitted that the case for the revised version relies on other merits than simplicity or elegance to make its claim good. It is not so smooth, nor so easy, nor, on the whole, so pretty as the older form. But it is nearly always richer and more alive. Abstractions give place to sharp definite images, loose vague phrases to close-locked significances. We can find a fair example of this in *The Madonna of the Future,*[25] a tale first published in 1879. In the original version one of the sentences runs: "His professions, somehow, were all half professions, and his allusions to his work and circumstances left something dimly ambiguous in the background." In the New York Edition this has become: "His professions were practically somehow, all masks and screens, and his personal allusions as to his ambiguous background mere wavings of the dim lantern." In some passages it would be hard to deny a gain of beauty as well as of significance. There is, for instance, a sentence in the earlier account of Newman's silent renunciation of his meditated revenge in the Cathedral of Notre Dame: "He sat a long time: he heard far-away bells chiming off, at long intervals, to the rest of the world." In the definitive edition of *The American* the passage has become: "He sat a long time; he heard far-away bells chiming off into space, at long intervals, the big bronze syllables of the Word."

A paragraph from *Four Meetings,*[26] a tale worked over with extreme care, will give a fair idea of the general effect of the revision. It records a moment of the final Meeting, when the helplessly indignant narrator is watching poor Caroline ministering to the vulgar French cocotte who has imposed herself on the hospitality of the innocent little New Englander.

"At this moment," runs the passage of 1879, "Caroline Spencer came out of the house bearing a coffee pot on a little tray. I noticed that on her way from the door to the table she gave me a single quick vaguely appealing glance. I wondered what it signified; I felt that it

25. Serialized in *Atlantic Monthly* March 1873; published in *A Passionate Pilgrim and Other Tales* (Boston: Osgood, 1875) and in *The Madonna of the Future and Other Tales* (London: Macmillan, 1879); included in vol. 13 of the New York Edition.
26. Serialized in *Scribner's Monthly,* November 1877; published in *Daisy Miller* (London: Macmillan, 1879); included in vol. 16 of the New York Edition.

signified some sort of half-frightened longing to know what, as a man of the world who had been in France, I thought of the Countess. It made me extremely uncomfortable. I could not tell her that the Countess was very possibly the runaway wife of a little hairdresser. I tried, suddenly, on the contrary, to show a high consideration for her."

This "particular vision" registered on re-perusal reveals states of mind much more definite than these wonderings and longing and vague appeals.

"Our hostess moreover at this moment came out of the house, bearing a coffee-pot and three cups on a neat little tray. I took from her eyes, as she approached us, a brief but intense appeal—the mute expression, as I felt, conveyed in the hardest little look she had yet addressed me, of her longing to know what as a man of the world in general and of the French world in particular, I thought of these allied forces so encamped on the stricken field of her life. I could only 'act,' however, as they said at North Verona, quite impenetrable—only make no answering sign. I couldn't imitate, much less could I frankly utter, my inward sense of the Countess's probable past, with its measure of her virtue, value and accomplishments, and of the limits of the consideration to which she could properly pretend. I couldn't give my friend a hint of how I myself personally 'saw' her interesting pensioner—whether as the runaway wife of a too-jealous hairdresser or of a too-morose pastry-cook, say; whether as a very small bourgeoise, in fine, who had vitiated her case beyond patching up, or even some character of the nomadic sort, less edifying still. I couldn't let in, by the jog of a shutter, as it were, a hard informing ray and then, washing my hands of the business, turn my back for ever. I could on the contrary but save the situation, my own at least, for the moment, by pulling myself together with a master hand and appearing to ignore everything but that the dreadful person between us *was* a 'grande dame.'"

Anyone genuinely interested in "the how and the whence and the why these intenser lights of experience come into being and insist on shining,"[27] will find it a profitable exercise to read and compare the old and the new versions of any of the novels and tales first published during the 'seventies or 'eighties. Such a reader will be qualified to decide for himself between the opinions of an intrepid critic[28] that "all the

27. Preface to *The Golden Bowl,* second sentence of paragraph 11.
28. Rebecca West, *Henry James* (London: Nisbet and Co., 1916); see Diary B, entry for Tuesday, 1 August 1916, and note 31.

works have been subjected to a revision which in several cases, notably *Daisy Miller* and *Four Meetings,* amounts to their ruin," and their writer's confidence that "I shouldn't have breathed upon the old catastrophes and accidents, the old wounds and mutilations and disfigurements wholly in vain . . . I have prayed that the finer air of the better form may sufficiently seem to hang about them and gild them over—at least for readers, however few, at all *curious* of questions of air and form."[29]

VI 🐎 Explanatory prefaces and elaborate revisions, short stories and long memories, were far from being the complete tale of literary labour during the last eight years of Henry James's life. A new era for English drama was prophesied in 1907. Led by Miss Horniman,[30] advocates of the repertory system were marching forward, capturing one by one the intellectual centres of the provinces. In London, repertory seasons were announced in two West-end theatres. Actor-managers began to ask for "non-commercial" plays and when their appeal reached Henry James it evoked a quick response.[31] The theatre had both allured and repelled him for many years, and he had already been the victim of a theatrical misadventure. His assertions that he wrote plays solely in the hope of making money[32] should not, I think, be taken as the complete explanation of his dramas. It is pretty clear that he wrote plays because he wanted to write them, because he was convinced that his instinct for

29. Preface to *The Golden Bowl,* first half of paragraph 15.

30. Annie Elizabeth Fredericka Horniman (1860–1937), a well-educated woman and confirmed feminist, was responsible, personally and financially, for the founding of the Abbey Theatre in Dublin in December 1904; her purchase of the Gaiety Theatre in Manchester marked the beginning, in April 1908, of the repertory movement in England.

31. For James's second theatrical period and an account of the "theatrical misadventure" mentioned at the end of the next sentence, the public failure of *Guy Domville* in January 1895, see Leon Edel, ed., *The Complete Plays of Henry James,* rev. ed. (Philadelphia: Lippincott, 1991).

32. In a letter to his brother William, 16 May 1890 (and elsewhere), he refers to his venture into the theater as prompted by "a religious and deliberate view of gain" (*The Letters of Henry James,* ed. Percy Lubbock, 2 vols. [New York: Charles Scribner's Sons, 1992], I, 162). Lubbock denies this motive in his introduction to section IV of the *Letters* (see p. 144). James had confided to his notebooks, 12 May 1889, that his venture was "for the sake of my pocket, my material future" (*Complete Notebooks,* 52); certainly his motives were mixed.

dramatic situations could find a happy outlet in plays, because writing
for the stage is a game rich in precise rules and he delighted in the multiplication of technical difficulties, and because he lived in circles more
addicted to the intelligent criticism of plays than to the intelligent criticism of novels. The plays he wrote in the early 'nineties are very careful exercises in technique. They are derived straight from the light
comedies of the Parisian stage, with the difference that in the 'nineties,
for all their advertised naughtiness, there were stricter limits on the
free representation of Parisian situations on English stages than there
are to-day. In *The Reprobate,*[33] a play successfully produced a few years
ago by the Stage Society, the lady whose hair has changed from black to
red and from red to gold is the centre of the drama, she holds the key
to the position, but all her complicating effect depends upon the past—
pasts being allowed on every stage comparative license of reference.
The compromising evidence is all a matter of old photographs and letters, and the play loses its vividness whatever it may gain in respectability. Nobody knew better than the author that *The Reprobate* was not a
good play. Terror of being cut forbade him to work on a subject of
intrinsic importance. With another hour guaranteed, a playwright
might attempt anything, but "he does not get his hour, and he will
probably begin by missing his subject. He takes, in his dread of compli-
cation, a minor one, and it's heavy odds that the minor one, with the
habit of small natures, will prove thankless."

Other early plays had been converted into novels or tales and so
published. One of these, written originally for Miss Ellen Terry[34] but
never produced by her, had appeared as an incongruous companion to

33. Not produced in James's lifetime; published with *The Album* in *Theatricals: Second Series* (London: Osgood, McIlvaine, 1894), and in *Complete Plays.*
34. Ellen Terry (1848–1928), famous British actress; the play, *Summersoft,* neither
produced nor published during James's lifetime, is in *Complete Plays;* Johnston Forbes
Robertson (1853–1937), British actor-manager; Gertrude Elliot, American actress
and Forbes Robertson's wife. "The Turn of the Screw," serialized in *Collier's Weekly,*
January–April 1898, was published with "Covering End" (no serialization) in *The
Two Magics* (London: Heinemann; and New York: Macmillan, 1898). *The Passing of
the Third Floor Back* by the English playwright Jerome K. Jerome (1859–1927)
prompted James's observation that "Jesus Christ is the main character and of course
one had to realise that He's a formidable competition" (Bosanquet's diary, 22
August 1908).

The Turn of the Screw in the volume entitled *The Two Magics*. A few
attentive readers had seen the dramatic possibilities of *Covering End*,
and when it was suggested to Henry James that he should convert it
into a three-act comedy for production by Mr. Forbes Robertson (as
he was then) and Miss Gertrude Elliot, he willingly consented. Flying
under a new flag, as *The High Bid*, the play was produced in London in
February, 1909, but only for a series of matinées, the prodigious success of *The Passing of the Third Floor Back* precluding the possibility of an
evening for any other production under the same management. Under
the inspiration of the repertory movement, other material was re-cast
for acting. *The Other House*[35] was re-dictated as a tragedy. *Owen
Wingrave* became *The Saloon*, a one-act play produced by Miss
Gertrude Kingston in 1910. Finally an entirely new three-act comedy,
The Outcry, was written round the highly topical subject of the sale of
art treasures to rich Americans. It was not produced during Henry
James's life. At the time when it should have been rehearsed he was ill
and the production was postponed. On his recovery, he went to the
United States for a year, and when he came back the day of repertory
performances had died in a fresh night of stars.

When *The Outcry* was given by the Stage Society in 1917, it was evident that the actors were embarrassed by their lines, for by 1909,
when the play was written, the men and women of Henry James could
talk only in the manner of their creator. His own speech, assisted by
the practice of dictating, had by that time become so inveterately characteristic that his questions to a railway clerk about a ticket or to a
fishmonger about a lobster, might easily be recognized as coined in the
same mint as his addresses to the Academic Committee of the Royal
Society of Literature. Apart from this difficulty of enunciating the
lines, *The Outcry* has all the advantages over the early plays. The characters are real and they act from adequate motives. The solution to the
presented problem, which requires, like most of the author's solu-
tions, a change of heart, is worked out with admirable art, without any

35. *The Other House* was serialized in the *Illustrated London News,* July–September
1896 and published in London by Heinemann and in New York by Macmillan, 1896;
the dramatization was not produced in James's lifetime. "Owen Wingrave"
appeared in *The Graphic,* November 1892, and was published in *The Private Life* (London: Osgood and McIlvaine, 1893) and in *The Wheel of Time* (New York: Harper,
1893). *The Saloon* opened in London in January 1911.

use of the mechanical shifts and stage properties needed in *The Repro-bate*. It is not very difficult to believe that if Henry James had been encouraged to go on writing plays he might have made a name as a dramatist, but the faithful may be forgiven for rejoicing that the play-wright was sacrificed to the novelist and critic.

VII 🐾. Many men whose prime business is the art of writing find rest and refreshment in other occupations. They marry or they keep dogs, they play golf or bridge, they study Sanskrit or collect postage stamps. Except for a period of ownership of a dachshund, Henry James did none of these things. He lived a life consecrated to the service of a jeal-ous, insatiable, and supremely rewarding goddess, and all his activities had essential reference to that service. He had a great belief in the virtues of air and exercise, and he was expert at making a walk of two or three miles last for as many hours by his habit of punctuating move-ment with frequent and prolonged halts for meditation or conversa-tion. He liked the exhilaration of driving in a motor-car, which gave him, he said, "a sense of spiritual adventure." He liked a communica-tive companion. Indeed the cultivation of friendships may be said to have been his sole recreation. To the very end of his life he was quick to recognize every chance of forming a friendly relation, swift to act on his recognition, and beautifully ready to protect and nourish the warm life of engendered affection. His letters, especially those writ-ten in his later years, are more than anything else great generous ges-tures of remembrance, gathering up and embracing his correspon-dents much as his talk would gather up his hearers and sweep them along on a rising flood of eloquence.

But that fine capacity for forming and maintaining a "relation" worked, inevitably, within definite limits. He was obliged to create impassable barriers between himself and the rest of mankind before he could stretch out his eager hands over safe walls to beckon and bless. He loved his friends, but he was condemned by the law of his being to keep clear of any really entangling net of human affection and exac-tion. His contacts had to be subordinate, or indeed ancillary, to the vocation he had followed with a single passion from the time when, as a small boy, he obtained a report from his tutor showing no great apti-tude for anything but a felicitous rendering of La Fontaine's fables into

English. Nothing could be allowed to interfere for long with the labour from which Henry James never rested, unless perhaps during sleep. When his "morning stint of inventive work" was over, he went forth to the renewed assault of the impressions that were always lying in wait for him. He was perpetually and mercilessly exposed, incessantly occupied with the task of assimilating his experience, freeing the pure workable metal from the base, remoulding it into new beauty with the aid of every device of his craft. He used his friends not, as some incompletely inspired artists do, as in themselves the material of his art, but as the sources of his material. He took everything they could give and he gave it back in his books. With this constant preoccupation, it was natural that the people least interesting to him were the comparatively dumb. To be "inarticulate" was for him the cardinal social sin. It amounted to a willful withholding of treasures of alien experience. And if he could extract no satisfaction from contemplating the keepers of golden silence, he could gain little more from intercourse with the numerous persons he dismissed from his attention as "simple organisms." These he held to be mere waste of any writer's time, and it was characteristic that his constant appreciation of the works of Mrs. Wharton,[36] was baffled by the popularity of *Ethan Frome,* because he considered that the gifted author had spent her labour on creatures too easily comprehensible to be worth her pains. He greatly preferred *The Reef,* where, as he said, "she deals with persons really fine and complicated."

We might arrive at the same conclusion from a study of the prefaces to the New York Edition. More often than not, the initial idea for a tale came to Henry James through the medium of other people's talk. From a welter of anecdote he could unerringly pick out the living nucleus for a reconstructed and balanced work of art. His instinct for selection was admirable, and he could afford to let it range freely among a profusion of proffered subjects, secure that it would alight on the most promising. But he liked to have the subjects presented with a little artful discrimination, even in the first instance. He was dependent on conversation, but it must be educated and up to a point intelligent conversation.

---

36. Edith Wharton (1862–1937), American novelist, a close friend of James's from 1900 to his death; James compared her novels *Ethan Frome* (New York: Scribner, 1911) and *The Reef* (New York: Appleton, 1912).

There is an early letter written from Italy in 1874,[37] in which he com-
plains of having hardly spoken to an Italian creature in nearly a year's
sojourn, "save washerwomen and waiters. This, you'll say, is my own
stupidity," he continues, "but granting this gladly, it proves that even a
creature addicted as much to sentimentalizing as I am over the whole
mise en scène of Italian life, doesn't find an easy initiation into what lies
behind it. Sometimes I am overwhelmed with the pitifulness of this
absurd want of reciprocity between Italy itself and all my rhapsodies
about it." Other wanderers might have found more of Italy in washerwomen and waiters, here guaranteed to be the true native article, than
in all the nobility of Rome or the Anglo-Americans of Venice, but that
was not Henry James's way. For him neither pearls nor diamonds fell
from the lips of waiters and washerwomen, and princesses never
walked in his world disguised as goosegirls.

Friendships are maintained by the communication of speech and letters. Henry James was a voluminous letter-writer and exhaustively
communicative in his talk upon every subject but one, his own work,
which was his own real life. It was not because he was indifferent to
what people thought of his books that he evaded discussion about them.
He was always touched and pleased by any evidence that he had been
intelligently read, but he never went a step out of his way to seek assurance. He found it safest to assume that nobody had read him, and he
liked his friends none the less for their incapacity. Meanwhile, the volumes of his published works—visible, palpable, readable proof of that
unceasing travail of the creative spirit which was always labouring
behind the barrier of his silence—piled themselves up year after year,
to be dropped on to the tables of booksellers and pushed on to the
shelves of libraries, to be bought and cherished by the faithful, ignored
by the multitude, and treated as a test of mental endurance by the kind
of person who organized the Browning Society. Fortunately for literature, Henry James did not lend himself to exploitation by any Jacobean
Society. Instead of inventing riddles for prize students, he scattered
about his pages a number of pregnant passages containing all the clues
that are needed for keeping up with him. It was his theory that if readers didn't keep up with him—as they admittedly didn't always—the

37. To Grace Norton (1834–1926), an old American friend, from Florence, dated
14 January 1874; see *Letters*, 1:36–37.

fault was entirely in their failure of attention. There are revelations in his books, just as he declared them to be in the works of Neil Paraday. "Extract the opinion, disengage the answer—these are the real acts of homage."[38]

VIII 🦋 From his familiar correspondence we need not hope to extract as considered an opinion or as definite an answer as from the novels, but his letters are extraordinarily valuable as sidelights, helping us to see how it happened that any man was able to progress along so straight a path from one end of his life to another. The two volumes of memories are clear evidence of the kind of temperamental make-up with which Henry James was gifted, the two volumes of letters[39] show how his life contributed to preserve and enhance his rare capacity for taking and keeping impressions. They show him too as unusually impervious to everything which is not an impression of visual images or a sense of a human situation. He was very little troubled by a number of ideas which press with an increasing weight upon the minds of most educated persons. Not until the outbreak of the great war was he moved to utter a forcible "opinion" about affairs outside his personal range. He was delightfully free from the common delusion that by grouping individuals in arbitrary classes and by twisting harmless adjectives into abstract nouns it is possible for us to think of more than one thing at a time and to conceive of qualities apart from their manifestation. What he saw he possessed; what he understood he criticized. But he never reckoned it to be any part of his business to sit in judgment on the deeds of men working in alien material for inartistic ends, or to speculate about the nature of the universe or the conflict or reconciliation of science with religion. He could let Huxley and Gladstone,[40] the combatant champions of Darwinism and orthodox theology, enrich the pages of a single letter without any ref-

---

38. Paraday is the novelist-hero of "The Death of the Lion"; the quotation is from the middle of part V of the story.

39. Lubbock's edition, published by Scribner in 1920.

40. Thomas Henry Huxley (1825–95), British biologist and writer, and William Ewart Gladstone (1809–98), British statesman, four times prime minister of England between 1868 and 1894; see letter to William James, 29 March 1877, on Huxley, *Letters*, 1:52, on Gladstone, 1:53.

erence to their respective beliefs. "Huxley is a very genial, comfort-able being . . . But of course my talk with him is mere amiable gen-eralities." Of Gladstone there is little more, but again the personal impression is the thing sought. "I was glad of a chance to feel the 'per-sonality' of a great political leader—or as G. is now thought here even, I think, by his partisans, ex-leader. That of Gladstone is very fascinating—his urbanity extreme—his eye that of a man of genius—and his apparent self-surrender to what he is talking of without a flaw. He made a great impression on men." One would like to know what the subject was to which Gladstone had surrendered himself in his talk with this entranced young American, who must surely for his part, have been as much reduced conversationally to "mere amiable generalities" as on the occasion of his meeting Huxley. It is difficult to think of a single likely point of contact between the minds of Glad-stone and Henry James. But that, for delicacy of registration, was an advantage. The recording instrument could perform its work with-out the hindrance of any distraction of attention from the man him-self to the matter of his speech, which did not presumably contain any germ for cultivation into fiction.

His nationality saved Henry James from the common English necessity of taking a side in the political game; and in the United States nobody of his world had expected him to be interested in politics. There is a pleasant account in *The Middle Years* of his blankness when he was asked at a London breakfast-table for "distinctness about General Grant's first cabinet, upon the formation of which the light of the newspaper happened then to beat." The question was embarrassing. "There were, it appeared, things of interest taking place in America, and I had had, in this absurd manner, to come to England to learn it: I had had over there on the ground itself no conception of any such mat-ter—nothing of the smallest interest, by any perception of mine, as I suppose I should still blush to recall, had taken place in America since the War." Nothing of any great public interest, by any perception of his, was to take place in Europe until the outbreak of another War at that time far beyond the range of speculation. But if cabinets and par-ties and politics were and remained outside the pale of his sensibility, he was none the less charmed by the customs of a country where Members of Parliament and Civil Servants could meet together for a leisurely breakfast, thus striking "the exciting note of a social order in which everyone wasn't hurled straight, with the momentum of rising, upon an office or a store."[41]

IX 🐾 Henry James came to England to admire. But his early reverence for the men and women of an island with so fine and ancient a historic tone as Great Britain soon faded. He had forgotten, in the first passion of acquaintance, that the English are born afresh in every generation and are about as new as young Americans, differing from them chiefly in having other forms of domestic and ecclesiastical architecture and smoother lawns to take for granted. He looked at old stone castles and Tudor brickwork, at great hanging eaves and immemorial gardens, and then he looked at the heirs of this heritage and listened intently for their speech. This was disappointing, partly because they spoke so little. "I rarely remember," he wrote when he had lived through several London months, "to have heard on English lips any other intellectual verdict (no matter under what provocation) than this broad synthesis 'so immensely clever.' What exasperates you is not that they can't say more, but that they wouldn't if they could."[42]

How different was this inarticulate world from the fine civilization of Boston, from the cultivated circle that gathered round Charles Eliot Norton at Shady Hill. To that circle he appealed for sympathy, complaining that he was "sinking into dull British acceptance and conformity. . . . I am losing my standard—my charming little standard that I used to think so high; my standard of wit, of grace, of good manners, of vivacity, of urbanity, of intelligence, of what makes an easy and natural style of intercourse! And this consequence of having dined out during the past winter 107 times!"[43] Great men, or at least the men with

---

41. Ulysses S. Grant (1822–85), Union general in the American Civil War and eighteenth president of the United States, 1869–77. In the second paragraph of the third section of *The Middle Years* James recalls this encounter; two paragraphs later he adds the observation on "the exciting note."

42. Letter from Great Malvern to William James, 8 March 1870. Lubbock correctly has a dash after "synthesis," which Bosanquet omits. The next sentence is important: "Ah, but they are a great people for all that" (1:27).

43. Norton (1827–1908), professor of the history of fine arts at Harvard from 1873, editor of the *North American Review* and *The Nation,* and friend of James from 1864; Shady Hill was his home in Cambridge, Massachusetts. James's letter from London, 8 June 1879, to Norton's sister Grace adds, two sentences later, "You must take that speech about my standard with a grain of salt" (1:69).

great names, swam into his ken and he condemned them. Ruskin was "weakness pure and simple." In Paris he found that he could "easily— more than easily—see all round Flaubert intellectually." A happy Sunday evening at Madame Viardot's provoked a curious reflection on the capacity of celebrated Europeans to behave absurdly and the incapacity of celebrated Americans to indulge in similar antics. "It was both strange and sweet to see poor Turgenev acting charades of the most extravagant description, dressed in old shawls, and masks, going on all fours, etc. The charades are their usual Sunday evening occupation and the good faith with which Turgenev, at his age and with his glories, can go into them is a striking example of the truth of that spontaneity which Europeans have and we have not. Fancy Longfellow, Lowell, or Charles Norton doing the like and every Sunday evening!"[44]

Whether or not all celebrated Americans behave with invariable decorum, the astonished spectator of Turgenev's performance had no temptation to "do the like." His appearance among a company of artists and writers gathered together in a country village during the late summer of 1886 has been characteristically recorded by Sir Edmund Gosse.[45] "Henry James was the only sedate one of us all— benign, indulgent, but grave, and not often unbending beyond a genial

44. John Ruskin (1819–1900), English author and art critic whom James met in 1869; James's letter, 26 March 1869, follows the quoted phrase with "I used the word, not invidiously, but scientifically" (1:20). Gustave Flaubert (1821–80), French novelist whom James met in 1875; James's letter of 11 April 1876, to his father, contains the phrase quoted and the subsequent account of the "Sundays en famille" (1:46). Pauline Viardot (1821–1910), French singer, had accepted into her ménage the Russian novelist Ivan Turgenev (1818–83), whom James met in November 1875. Henry Wadsworth Longfellow (1807–82), American poet, and James Russell Lowell, American writer and diplomat, were part of Norton's circle. The phrase "of the truth" was added following "striking example," although it does not appear in "The Record of Henry James"; that earlier version also seems fairer to Europeans—and indeed to James's opinion of them. In the 1920 essay the passage on Ruskin, Flaubert, et al. begins, "Nevertheless, he liked living in London because he could there be 'an observer in a place where there is most in the world to observe'" (see letter to Grace Norton, 7 August 1877, Letters, 1:54), and the subsequent paragraph offers a subtly different beginning: "How unlikely this interested commentator was to 'do the like' spontaneously, we may judge from Mr. Edmund Gosse's account of his appearance among a holiday-making company of artists and writers in . . . 1886."
45. Edmund Gosse (1849–1928), essayist, biographer, and finally librarian of the

chuckle. . . . It is remembered with what affability he wore a garland of flowers at a birthday feast, and even, nobly descending, took part one night in a cake-walk. But mostly, though not much our senior, he was serious, mildly avuncular, but very happy and unupbraiding."

By that time Henry James was at his ease in England. The inhabitants were no longer either gods or imbeciles. Through the general British fog he had perceived gleams of intelligence shining on his bewilderment. He was no longer wholly dependent on Boston for refreshment. He could fall back upon the company of Mr. Edmund Gosse and he had found a friend in R. L. Stevenson.[46] The little handful of Islanders possessed of a genuine interest in the art of letters and the criticism of life emerged from the obscurity, and he made out that, on the whole, there were perhaps as many civilized people in England as in his native land. Yet he was a little troubled about his position. He wondered, while he reviewed the past, whether the path he had so carefully chosen for himself was the right one, whether he might not have missed more by leaving the United States than he had gained by coming to England. He lamented, in a letter written to his brother William in 1899, that he had not had the kind of early experience that might have attached him to his own country. He earnestly advised a different treatment for his nephews. "What I most of all feel, and in the light of it conjure you to keep doing for them, is their being *à même* to contract local saturations and attachments in respect to their *own* great and glorious country, to learn, to strike roots into, its infinite beauty, as I suppose, and variety. . . . Its being their 'own' will double their *use* of it."[47]

It was only after a visit to America in 1904 that he found, on his return to Rye, that he had a home and a country.[48] He was able after

House of Lords, had been a friend of James's since 1876 and was one of his sponsors for British citizenship in 1915.

46. Robert Louis Stevenson (1850–94), Scottish novelist and essayist, and a friend of James's since 1884.

47. Letter of 22 April (*Letters,* 1:316).

48. James was on a lecture tour of America between August 1904 and July 1905; his subsequent publications (especially *The American Scene,* London: Chapman and Hall; and New York: Harper, 1907) indicate the extent of his alienation from his old home. But Bosanquet seems to have confused—or simply fused—his two return voyages to the United States; the second, six years later, confirmed his sense of home at Rye that she emphasizes here, and the next sentence of Bosanquet's text

this discovery to write to Mrs. Wharton that "your only drawback is not having the homeliness and the inevitability and the happy limitation and the affluent poverty, of a Country of your Own (comme moi, par exemple!)";[49] and he could declare after taking the oath of Allegiance to the King of England in 1915 that "I was really too associated before for any nominal change to matter. The process has only shown me what I virtually *was*—so that it's rather disappointing in respect to acute sensation. I *haven't* any."[50] Associated he certainly was, allied by innumerable sympathies and affections to the adopted country. But he was never really English or American or even Cosmopolitan.[51] And it is too difficult to suppose that even if he had passed all his youth in New England and contracted all the local saturations and attachments he urged for his nephews he could ever have melted comfortably into American uniformity. He, who took nothing in the world for granted, could surely never have taken New England for granted.

To-day, with the complete record before us—the novels, criticisms, biographies, plays and letters—we can understand how little those international relations that engaged Henry James's attention mattered to his genius. Wherever he might have lived and whatever human interactions he might have observed, he would in all probabil-

---

refers to a letter of 1912: see note 49. Shortly after regaining Lamb House he wrote to his friend George A. James (12–13 August 1911): "I find I take up my old traditions on this small spot . . . with remarkable facility, and I should indeed even say with quiet ecstasy—. . . My old garden-walls are crooked with purple age, and the little russet townroofs that peep between the trees show me a few chimney pots as of the time of the Tudors. But George Gammon (my very gardener's name is Shakespearean to me again), has kept my lawn almost vivid."

49. Letter of 4–9 December 1912.

50. Letter to Edmund Gosse, 26 July 1915—the day of his taking the Oath of Allegiance (*Letters,* 2:492).

51. As early as 29 October 1888 James unburdened himself to brother William on this topic: "I am deadly weary of the whole 'international' state of mind—so that I *ache,* at times, with fatigue at the way it is constantly forced upon one as a sort of virtue or obligation. I can't look at the English and American worlds, or feel about them, save as a big Anglo-Saxon total . . . I aspire to write in such a way that it would be impossible to an outsider to say whether I am, at a given moment, an American writing about England or an Englishman writing about America (dealing as I do with both countries) . . . I should be exceedingly proud of it, for it would be highly civilized" (*Letters: 1883–1895,* vol. 3, ed. Leon Edel [Cambridge: Harvard University Press, 1980], 244). See above, p. 132.

ity have reached much the same conclusions that he arrived at by the
way of America, France, and England. When he walked out of the
refuge of his study into the world and looked about him, he saw a place
of torment, where creatures of prey perpetually thrust their claws into
the quivering flesh of the doomed, defenceless children of light. He
had the abiding comfort of an inner certainty (and perhaps he did bring
that from New England) that the children of light had an eternal advantage; he was aware to the finest fibre of his being that the "poor sensitive gentlemen" he so numerously treated possessed a treasure that
would outlast all the glittering paste of the world and the flesh; he
knew that nothing in life mattered compared with spiritual decency.

We may conclude that the nationalities of his betrayed and triumphant victims are not an important factor. They may equally well
be innocent Americans maltreated by odious Europeans, refined
Europeans fleeced by unscrupulous Americans, or young children of
any race exposed to evil influences. The essential fact is that wherever
he looked Henry James saw fineness apparently sacrificed to gross-
ness, beauty to avarice, truth to a bold front. He realised how constantly the tenderness of growing life is at the mercy of personal
tyranny and he hated the tyranny of persons over each other. His novels are a repeated exposure of this wickedness, a reiterated and passionate plea for the fullest freedom of development, unimperilled by
reckless and barbarous stupidity.

He was himself most scrupulously careful not to exercise any tyran-
nical power over other people. The only advice he ever permitted
himself to offer to a friend was a recommendation to "let your soul
live." Towards the end of his days his horror of interfering, or seem-
ing to interfere, with the freedom of others, became so overpowering
that it was a misery for him to suspect that the plans of his friends
might be made with reference to himself. Much as he enjoyed seeing
them, he so disliked to think that they were undertaking the discomfort of voyages and railway journeys in order to be near him that he
would gladly have prevented their start if he could. His Utopia was an
anarchy where nobody would be responsible for any other human
being but only for his own civilised character. His circle of friends will
easily recall how finely Henry James had fitted himself to be a citizen
of this commonwealth.

Excerpts from the Bosanquet Diary

I want this diary (as far as it goes) to be a sort of general account of one's reactions at the time of writing.

—*Theodora Bosanquet, 30 September 1914*

Diary A

🐎 Professional Relations of Theodora Bosanquet with
Henry James and His Family (WITH SUPPLEMENTARY LETTERS)

Thursday, 22 August 1907. I went, as usual, to work[1]—to Conduit street
by bus—as I felt sick and headachy and not inclined to brave the noise
of the tube. The bus was very slow—but pleasant and did really land me
near Conduit st. in good time. Coast erosion proofs galore to read.

But the event of the day was Mr. Henry James' visit. He called on
Miss Petherbridge at about 12 and after about half an hour—when I
was fearfully cold with nervousness—I was sent for. I wore a white
shirt and green skirt, belt and tie—a business-like and, I hoped,
becoming costume.—

He is like Coleridge—in figure—one feels he ought to be wearing
a flowered waistcoat—very expansive—"unrestrained," in the lower
part. He wore green trousers and a blue waistcoat with a yellow sort
of check on it and a black coat—that was rather a shock. I'd imagined
him as always very correctly dressed—in London. He is bald—except
for tufts of not very grey hair at the sides. His eyes, grey I think, are
exactly what I should expect—but the rest of his face is too fat. He
talks slowly but continuously—I found it hard to get in any words of
my own. But he is *most* kind and considerate—and asked me to go
down for a day some time to lunch with him and see possible rooms.
He also said he could promise to lend me as many books as I could possibly want. He says he is often very slow in dictating—and I can have
work or a book to amuse me while he is evolving sentences! He was
careful to impress upon me the danger of boredom.—

---

1. Miss Petherbridge's secretarial office and employment agency. See opening lines
of *Henry James at Work*.

He hasn't the self-possession I should have expected—but he seems most kind and nice—and so—absolutely unassuming.

[Thursday], 10 October [1907], Rye. Got off by the 11 train—and had an uneventful journey to Rye—reading "Cornhill" and "Queens of the Renaissance"—a quite good book. Mr. James met me—and a grimy working man[2] took my boxes. Mr. James apologised for the grime— said "He ought not to have shown himself like that." We walked to my rooms—Marigold Cottage[3]—the talk being slightly constrained. He talked of the days when he used to go to see "dear old Burne Jones" in the North End Rd. in a house (I think) once inhabited by Richardson.[4]

Mrs. Holland, my landlady, seems very pleasant and kind, and my lunch was excellent. After some subsequent unpacking I went to Mr. James' house and he introduced me to his typewriter—which I inspected for an hour or so—a brand new Remington and very complicated—or so it seemed to me. Back here to tea feeling horribly desolate and wrote letters—in a gloomy strain. These rooms are nice enough—as lodgings—but oh they're not a patch on my beloved flat.

Friday, 11 October 1907. After a post-breakfast stroll where I was mainly struck by the pretty view downwards towards the south-east over the levels—with the masts of the sailing boats marking Rye Harbour, I repaired, at 10.15 to Mr. James's house. He let me in—and showed me shelves of books from which I might borrow—it's *awfully* nice of him. Then I went upstairs to his working room—a little square room—with two windows—one S.E., the other S.W. I think—more books—easy chairs and a bureau on which the machine stood. He is dictating prefaces to a revised edition of his earlier works and this morning was devoted to one on "The Tragic Muse"[5]—in the tone of a personal reminiscence. He dictates considerably—slowly and very

---

2. George Gammon, James's devoted gardener.
3. At the top (east end) of Mermaid Street on the north side, just around the corner from Lamb House. See photo section, p. 8.
4. Sir Edward Burne-Jones (1833–98), English painter, whom James met in 1869. Samuel Richardson (1689–1761), English novelist, author of epistolary novels (*Pamela, Clarissa,* etc.).
5. Novel published in 1890 in New York and Boston by Houghton, and in London by Macmillan; vols. 7 and 8 in the Scribner New York Edition.

clearly—giving all the punctuations and often the spelling. I was abominably slow and clumsy—but he was very kind—even complimentary though he admitted that he hoped I should soon go a little faster. He sat in a chair at first—then paced about, smoking—finishing soon after half past one—when I had the joy of exploring some of his book shelves—and carried off two books "For Better? For Worse?" by G. E. W. Russell,[6] and a book on Meredith's poetry by Trevelyan[7]—given to Henry James by Meredith himself—so presumably worth reading. I hardly know if I dare ask for the poems—as Mr. James' Merediths are all so beautiful. My luncheon over, I dipped into the books, then set off for a walk, calling at a house agent's to enquire if there were any vacant houses near, such as would be suitable for Aylmer. He gave me three addresses, and I walked out to look at the outside of one of the houses near a village called Iden. The house is hideous—just like a doll's house architecturally, and won't, I'm afraid, do at all. Back to tea and wrote to Nora—posted it—read—supper—more reading—such is the day. A friend of Mrs. Goolden's, a Mrs. Granville Bradley[8] called while I was out—very kindly.

Mr. James assumes complete ignorance of any literary knowledge on the part of his amanuensis. He told me that "The Newcomes" was in one word, and that it was by Thackeray!

Friday, 8 November 1907. After the morning's work, as we neared the conclusion of the play, I said I hoped it would be acted by some one with sufficient personal charm—and he plunged into the history of it. It was written about 12 years ago—at Ellen Terry's request as a one-act play for her to produce in America.[9] She was delighted with it—

6. *"For Better? For Worse?" Notes on Social Change* (London, 1902) by the British writer and politician George William Erskine Russell (1853–1919).

7. George Meredith (1828–1909), English novelist and poet, a friend of James's since 1878. *The Poetry and Philosophy of George Meredith* by the British historian George Macaulay Trevelyan (1876–1962) was published in London in 1906.

8. Wife of the English writer Arthur Granville Bradley (1850–1943), who published many works on British colonies in the New World (Canada and Virginia) and travel literature and a fellow walker-about-Rye with James; they lived in Red Cottage on the north side of Rye where Bosanquet met their daughter "Nellie."

9. Ellen Terry (1848–1928), famous British actress, asked James for a play in 1895; he wrote the one-act *Summersoft* for her, but she never used it; in 1898 he recovered the script and turned it into the short story "Covering End" (1898).

jumped about and "behaved in an Ellen Terryish way"—took it off to America and *didn't* produce it. A few years afterwards—wanting a story to be made into a book with "The Turn of the Screw"—he wrote to Ellen Terry and told her he was going to print it—"embedded in a certain amount of commentary"—and so he did. Then Forbes-Robertson who was then acting with Mrs. Patrick Campbell[10] wrote and said—did he know there was a play in it!—and might he play it *with* Mrs. P.C. and Mr. James said "No." George Alexander also wrote to ask if *he* might—with Fay Davis.[11] So the matter dropped. Now Ellen Terry [is] too old—incapable of learning a part. Forbes-Robertson married to a young American actress[12]—sufficiently pretty and of whose talents *he* has a great opinion wrote to say he was still faithful to the play and would Mr. James allow him to do it with *her.* Mr. James replied that he would, but it was long as a one-act play, and would need some cutting—whereupon F.R. rejoined that he didn't want a single word cut and suggested it as a possible three-act play, and Mr. James, looking it over, saw that this *was* possible—so that's how it's written. This I'm, of course, to "bury deep."

As he let me out I restored "An English Girl" and "Kipps." He said Hueffer[13] *ought* to be pronounced in the German way but round here people call him 'Hufer.' He also asked what I thought of "Kipps." He thinks himself it's the cleverest and most wonderful novel that's been published for several years! After lunch went a walk and enjoyed it. It was such a lovely afternoon—warm sunny and *clear*—there's been so

10. The British actor Johnston Forbes-Robertson (1853–1947) made his request in 1899. James then refused but agreed to his repeated request in 1907 and gave him the three-act *The High Bid.* Beatrice Stella Campbell (1865–1940), a beautiful and talented British actress who gained fame in *The Second Mrs. Tanqueray* (1893) and enjoyed enormous success as Eliza Doolittle with George Alexander in Shaw's *Pygmalion* (1914).

11. George Alexander (1858–1918), popular actor-manager of the St. James's Theatre in London; Fay Davis was an actress in Alexander's company.

12. Gertrude Elliott of Rockland, Maine, met Forbes-Robertson in 1900.

13. Ford Hermann Hueffer (1873–1939), important English novelist, changed his name to Ford Madox Ford in 1919; his novel *An English Girl* was published in 1907, and his critical biography *Henry James* was published in 1914. Bosanquet's diary entry for 5 November 1907: "Read Ford Madox Hueffer's 'An English Girl' which seems to me (am I 'obsessed'?) to owe a lot to Henry James's influence." *Kipps* (1905), a novel by H. G. Wells (1866–1946), a prolific English writer whom James admired.

thick a mist hanging about lately—it was nice to *see* things more. Read and did short-hand after tea till Mr. James passed some M.s.s. in through the window to be underlined.

Thursday, 12 December [1907]. I read this morning in the intervals the beginning of Fanny Burney's Diary.[14] I had no idea it was so entertaining a book, and how it reflects on *me*—how little I have been able to put Mr. James on these pages—even the 100th part as clearly as she puts the Streatham party. I do wonder that she *didn't* succeed at plays. Indeed these past days there has been nothing to relate of my own great Man, who paralyses me more and more. We've worked in silence—broken, of course, by the dictated sentences. Today he came round at about 3 o'clock to pay me my dues and enquire what my plans for Xmas were. I said I didn't want to go away, and he seemed rather perplexed, and sat silent a bit—so I said "Of course I *can* go away if you like," and he said "Oh no—no—I think, in fact, yes I can manage so quite well. If you were going away—it's rather nice to have a few 'outside' mornings to get on with my revision. When you're here, I don't like to tell you not to come—but I think that will really do best perhaps—and then, after Xmas, if you think you can face it, I propose to stay here till the end of February, if there isn't too much east wind—if you can put up with it—I daresay I may stay on even later myself, but I shall be glad to have a rest by then." I felt, at the end of it all, the most hopeless fool, as I always do with him—however I'm off to tea with the Bradleys and shall hope there to recover some better opinion of myself.

And I went—and did. Mrs. Bradley was in bed with a liver chill and Mr. B. in the other room doctoring a child—so Miss Bradley entertained me alone for some time and then Mrs. Prentice, a very nice lively little woman, appeared. I outstayed her and had more conversation with Miss Bradley—was asked to tea next Sunday and dinner on Christmas day and then departed. Felt most invigorated all the evening and was inspired to write to Mrs. Wason.

---

14. Frances Burney, Mme Alexandre d'Arblay (1752–1840), British novelist and diarist. James had in his library *Diary and Letters of Madame D'Arblay* (London: Henry Colborn, 1842–46).

Thursday, 19 December [1907]. Re-dictation of first part of play,[15] still in the garden room, at a furiously high temperature owing to the pipes being "full on." Mr. James remarked that the "hot house atmosphere should cause the flowers of my genius to expand." I wasn't very comfortable at the table there—legs too long to get comfortably under it—so he sent for another table. I read Edmund Gosse's "Father and Son"[16] and carried it off to finish—it's most interesting, and inspired me to begin my own autobiography, not that *it's* one. Mrs. Howes came in in the afternoon to ask me to dinner on Xmas day, and like a fool I half promised to go, and I *don't* want to go. I could so easily have made out that the Bradleys' invitation was for the evening too. She also warned me against a certain Mrs. Cory who may call! Then I went out, just in the town, and then home to tea and shorthand, washed hair—voilà tout!

Sunday, 22 December [1907]. Mr. James *is* working hard on the "Owen Wingrave" play. He has had nearly a morning's work ready prepared for dictation the last few days so we go at quite a pace. I don't like the garden room so well as the other—it's too stuffy, with the hot water pipes and no open windows.

Friday, 27 December [1907]. I hate working in that hot water heated garden room—which is all the comment to be made *re* today's work.

Friday, 7 August [1908]. "William"[17] and "Henry" both went to London for the day so I spent the morning copying the last preface—also putting on a new ribbon—a messy job, but I was allowed hot water, and washed my hands in Mr. James' room—*such* a nice room, pan-

---

15. *The Saloon,* produced in London in January 1911, was an adaptation of his short story "Owen Wingrave" (1892); see entry for 22 December 1907 in this diary.

16. Gosse (1849–1928), British writer and finally librarian of the House of Lords, met James in 1879; James's library included the 1907 edition of Gosse's novel.

17. William James (1842–1910) came over to England in the spring of 1908; he gave the Hibbert Lectures at Oxford University in May and spent the summer at Lamb House with his wife and visits from their children well into the fall—to the evident delight of Bosanquet.

eled, all quite simple, photographic reproductions on the walls. Two *charming* little silver candlesticks by the bed. A very good old mirror against the wall.

Monday, 21 September [1908]. Play continued and Act II ended.[18] I called on the Powles in afternoon—meant to see Mrs. Ford[19] but met Nellie [Bradley] in the town and went back to tea with her instead—also stayed to supper after which I read to her. While we were out with the dogs after tea we met Mr. James and his brother who turned and walked back with us, H.J with Nellie, W.J. with me. He said how *very* fond he has got of this country with its soft harmonious colouring and of how sorry he was to be going away. He *is* a charming man—there's something so simple and fresh about him somehow.

Saturday, 26 September [1908]. Play in morning, but before that I saw Mrs. William James and her son and daughter[20] off and received the most friendly invitations to go and see them if ever I was in America—then went a stroll with Nellie and the dogs. In afternoon went to Red Cottage,[21] sat in Nellie's room and read to her (Greek Religious Teachers) till tea—we went for a stroll after and I stayed to supper.

Thursday, 26 November [1908]. After a frenzied morning of striving to "boil down" "The Tree Top,"[22] Mr. James disclosed schemes for going away to me—next week will be much broken. Nellie came up at 4 and we started learning Italian! Tea at Mr. James'.

---

18. James was converting his novel of 1896, *The Other House,* into a play of the same title; it was not produced.

19. Mr. and Mrs. Francis Ford (he was a music critic) of nearby Wittersham were good friends of James.

20. Alice H. née Gibbens (1849–1922); the third Henry James (1879–1947)—called "Harry"; and Margaret Mary "Peggy" James (1887–1952).

21. A capacious dwelling on the northern fringes of Rye, beyond the railway line.

22. That is, "The Top of the Tree," published as "The Velvet Glove," *English Review,* March 1909. James was responding to a request for a story from *Harper's Monthly;* the response resulted in "the sheaf of tales" (as Bosanquet says at the end of section II, *Henry James at Work*) collected in *The Finer Grain,* 1910—all except "A Round of Visits" (*English Review,* April–May 1910).

Saturday, 12 December [1908]. What shocking gaps! However the tide of life flows smoothly on. Mr. James works steadily—at present on a quite short story for Harper's.[23] He hasn't talked much lately apart from his work.

Tuesday, 15 December [1908]. Mr. James wrestling with the problem of redistribution of three volumes of short tales—to make up four. Also with the consequent alterations in Prefaces. I went back for extra work after tea.

Thursday, 17 December [1908]. Wet. Mr. James going on with "short" story ["Crapy Cornelia"] for Harper's which extends mightily—and is, I think, dull.

Thursday, 24 December [1908]. After an hour or so's work Mr. James left off as he had to pack up to go to Wittersham, where he and his nephew Alec[24] spend Xmas with the Fords. He presented me with a glovebox, which rather annoyed me—I think he might have chosen a little more carefully, or given me a book. The glove box is just the sort of thing one would give an illiterate house-keeper. However he meant it very kindly I've no doubt. I went in the town afterwards where I met Nellie and we strolled round doing errands and looked in at the Studio.[25] Didn't do much in the afternoon. Nellie came up to supper and I read "Justice and Liberty" to her.[26]

Saturday, 2 January [1909]. James at work on another short story,[27] which promises very well indeed. Nellie came up to tea and I went to supper at Red Cottage.

---

23. "Crapy Cornelia," *Harper's Monthly,* October 1909.
24. Alexander Robertson James (1890–1946), William's youngest.
25. In Watchbell St. and adjacent to the southwest corner of the Lamb House garden, an annex to the property, was the "studio" in which Bosanquet's predecessor as James's secretary, Mary Weld (d. 1953), and her friend Marion Lane briefly set up a bookbindery and in fact bound some of James's books.
26. Published in 1908 by Goldsworthy Lowes Dickinson (1862–1932), Fellow of King's College, Cambridge, classical scholar and liberal political thinker.
27. "Mora Montravers," *English Review,* August–September 1909.

Sunday, 3 January [1909]. Mr. James had done a lot of work on his story last night and we raced along. He says he wants to do three or four, and finds his only plan is to write them himself—it keeps him more within bounds—and *then* dictate them. Hope he'll remember to pay me for copying them! He forgot the last. He is so kind in providing chocolates for me!

Friday, 8 January [1909]. Mr. James began another story.[28] I felt headachy all day, slumbered over the fire in afternoon. Nellie came in for a little and I read the "Hound of Heaven" and another of Thompson's[29] poems to her.

Friday, 22 January [1909]. Went to Mr. James after tea. He received, while I was there, a letter from Forbes Robertson giving dates of matinees for "The High Bid" beginning Feb. 18th—which I'm to go up [to London] for. No clothes! What shall I do? Borrow, perhaps, from Nora!

Thursday, 18 February [1909]. . . . met Nellie at His Majesty's [Theatre] for the 1st performance of "The High Bid" in the afternoon. It was really on the whole very adequately acted—Gertrude Elliott in particular was a real success, and the "Cora" excellent. F.R. himself as Yule I didn't so much care for.

Saturday, 25 December [1909]. Nellie and I (domiciled some months since at the Studio) passed a peaceful day reading and writing. In the evening we arrayed ourselves—she in a charmingly pretty blue gown and I in old black togs—and went to dine at Lamb House. Mr. Bailey Saunders[30] staying there. I disliked what I saw of him yesterday, but this evening he was much more pleasant—quite a good talker, and often witty. Mr. James was delightfully genial and nice. Nellie and I each found glove-boxes on our plates! He looked "real lovely" in a cracker mask after dinner—we all did, but he was the best! They were pleasant, benevolent sort of masks only down to the mouth with a

---

28. "The Bench of Desolation," *Putnam's,* October–December 1910.
29. Francis Thompson (1859–1907), English poet.
30. T. Bailey Saunders, British journalist.

hole for the nose. Mr. James' most successful one was a fat old lady with side curls, which made us so hilarious that he had to send for a shaving-glass to see himself in it. "Why," he propounded, "don't we all wear masks and change them as we do our clothes?" Why not, indeed—it would be almost as good as changing one's personality. Should have enjoyed it more if I hadn't had a headache. Mr. James made many enquiries re the King's Cross Mansions in which Nellie and I had taken a flat. I think he quite entertains the idea of taking one himself—just to work in.

LAMB HOUSE

RYE, SUSSEX

23rd January 1910

Dear Mr. James,[31]

It has struck me that a line from an independent source may be some relief to you in case you are feeling anxious about Mr. Henry James' health at this juncture[32]—which is my excuse for writing you this little note. I interviewed Dr. Skinner[33] this morning, with encouraging results. He says that he considers Mr. James much better, and there is absolutely no cause for anxiety. He has been persuaded, since yesterday, to deliver himself into the hands of the Doctor and Nurse completely, and is being kept in bed and fed every two hours—a course of treatment which has been almost immediately beneficial! His own method, you know, has been to eat little or nothing and go for immense walks, which has perhaps had something to with the many and puzzling relapses he has had lately.

I shall be leaving Rye myself on Tuesday, as Mr. James has no use for an amanuensis for the next few months. (This is not on account of his illness, he had arranged to work by himself for some little time in any case.) But if you should at any time want "independent information" the Doctor—Dr. Skinner, Mountsfield, Rye—could of course supply it.

---

31. William's eldest, Henry "Harry," back in the United States.
32. James was suffering from a combination of digestive disorders and persistent depression that was in great part due to the poor sales of his New York Edition. William sent Harry over at the end of February to arrange medical attention for him.
33. Dr. Ernest Skinner, James's local physician.

With kind regards to Mrs. James and yourself believe me your very truly

Theodora Bosanquet

LAMB HOUSE

March 2d. 1910

Dear Miss Bosanquet,[34]

Alas, I have been making no "strides"—except backward, and things have been very bad with me; too bad for me to write or make any sign. In short I am still having a very difficult and uphill time, with the one mitigation that one of my Boston nephews, the eldest,[35] has just come out from America to be with me, and is a blessed support. But the end is not yet—nor do I see it in sight. I got up this a.m. from 9 days again in bed. I thank you very kindly for your letter. Everything seems "hung up," blighted and indefinitely postponed. There can be no production of The Outcry[36] without my personal participation at preparation and rehearsal—and till there is a possibility of that no calculating. There can even be no casting of the piece without my presence in London. So all that is dark. History is strangely written—I don't know where, or how, you heard of my stay at Wittersham! I have no more been able to stay at Wittersham than in Kamschatka! I hope your London and your establishment "work," through everything; and I greet Miss Bradley very kindly. But I am sorry to be able to give you no more brilliant news of your poor old blighted

Henry James

P.S. There is a plan for my somehow seeing a very high authority— the highest, doubtless—next week.[37]

---

34. This letter is handwritten in pencil.

35. Nephew Harry arrived at Lamb House, Rye, on 24 February 1910.

36. James's play intended for the repertory program planned by the Scottish playwright James M. Barrie (1860–1937) and others to be produced by the American Charles Frohman (1860–1915). The death of King Edward VII on 6 May 1910 effectively ended the plan, and The Outcry was not produced in James's lifetime, but he converted the scenario into a novel of the same title (London: Methuen; and New York: Scribner, 1911) with great success.

37. Harry took James up to London on 12 March 1910 to see the Canadian physician Sir William Osler (1849–1919), the "father of psychosomatic medicine"; after two visits Osler found him physically sound but suffering from melancholia—what brother William then called "a nervous breakdown."

Saturday, 7 May [1910]. Black-bordered "Times" announcing the King's death[38]—which comes to one as a real personal grief— changed into black garments and went to work. Met Nora at 1 and we lunched at Vienna Café—her birthday. Afterwards we went to St. James's—just in time to see the carriage returning from Buckingham Palace with the new King and Queen. We then followed the Horse Artillery to the Horse Guard's parade and listened to as much as our heads could stand of the 68 minutes guns fired in the late King's honour. Then went back to St. James's Palace and saw the Privy Councillor and Lord Mayor going to the meeting at 4 o'clock—after which we went and had tea—returning however in good time to see them leaving and to have a good view of King George as he drove back to Marlborough House—in Admiral's uniform. Nora went back after that but I walked round by Buckingham Palace where there were more crowds—partly waiting on the chance of King George going back there and partly to read the announcement of the King's death, which still hung on the railings, tied on by a bit of string.

I wandered along the Mall and up into St. Martin's Lane. In a second-hand bookshop I heard a stout cleric, a non-conformist minister, giving his views on the occurrence at great length. "What *shall* we do?" he asked, "What *shall* we do?" "Try to sell our books" suggested the shopman, but the other wouldn't be put off, but launched out into what *he* would like to do. At last, having bored the two shopmen with silence, he said "What did he die of?" whereupon one of the others revived and said "Cancer," going on to declare that it had been known for a long time that the King had been dangerously ill *much* longer than people had any idea of and that as to his having transacted business and given audiences the last two days "it's all lies—every word of it!" The good minister, though sensational enough himself, was *rather* staggered by this. I encountered him later in another bookshop. "Oh," he exclaimed, "this is an awful day—awful! *You* can't be doing much of a trade."

Dined at the Gourmet—then home to bed.

---

38. Edward VII (b. 1841) had reigned since the death of his mother, Queen Victoria, in 1901; his son, George V (1865–1936), succeeded him.

LAMB HOUSE

RYE, SUSSEX

August 4th 1910

Dear Miss Bosanquet,

All thanks for your very interesting letter. The "cut," all murdered, copy[39] hasn't come yet—and I fidget (at the disastrous possibilities of loss through gross carelessness in the theatre) while I wait for it. However, it will probably turn up—it won't have been destroyed. Meanwhile, at any rate, I shall be in town on Saturday, and wondering if by chance you may be *not* out of it, and if in that case I might come to see you on that day toward 4.30 o'clock. I lunch with the Protheros[40] in Bedford Square at 1.30—and shall be there some time—that is for a couple of hours. Might I come on from there to you, if you (and I hope Miss Bradley) aren't to be absent? The best thing would be if you could kindly let me have a word c/o G. W. Prothero Esq. 24 B.S., with "to await arrival" in the corner. I leave here tomorrow a.m. and sleep at Windsor[41]—but come up rather betimes on Saturday. I hope it may fortunately happen—! Yours very truly

Henry James

95 Irving House

Cambridge, Massachusetts[42]

May 14th 1911

Dear Miss Bosanquet,

You must have wondered endlessly at my graceless and thankless—as well as endless—silence.[43] I won't attempt to do more about the dreadful matter just now, however, than say that there has been all

---

39. His play *The Outcry,* which he had reluctantly cut at the urging of Harley Granville-Barker (1877–1946), British all-round man of the theater and with Barrie a prime mover in the repertory plan. The "copy" was to be used in transforming play into novel.

40. George Walter Prothero (1848–1922), English historian and president of the Royal Society of Literature, and his wife, Fanny, were near neighbors of James in Rye; their London home was in Bedford Square.

41. At Queen's Acre, home of Howard Sturgis (1855–1920), on the edge of Windsor Great Park.

42. The William James family home.

43. Still recovering from the blow of his brother's death, James also had a recurrence of the attack of "melancholia" he suffered just a year earlier in March 1910.

along a sad and strange inevitability in it, and that even while [I] have
myself brooded on that fact most gloomily I have been able to say to
myself that you would understand it, believe that my circumstances
and conditions somehow discouraged and hindered or at least ham-
pered my reporting of myself and that you would certainly hear
when—as soon as—such "inhibitions" should decline. Well, I am
happy to say that they *have* declined—though only at the slowest and
most backward rate, and I know at last sufficiently where I am to be
able to talk to you with some appeal as to the practical application of
my words. I have had an *interminably* difficult and depressing time—
that is the plain unvarnished tale; I felt that my not writing was the
best way of letting you know this—the best because the least dis-
agreeable and dreary and sympathy-invoking in yourself; and in fine
the general fact that when I reported myself "better" I immediately
became worse, and when I reported myself worse I immediately
became a bore and an affliction, resolved itself into the general necessity of staying my hand all round—inasmuch as I found I could never
let it get into motion without its appearing to report me *somehow*. Let
me hasten to add however that the situation has at last essentially
changed for the better—I'm afraid I even *now* shouldn't be writing if
it hadn't. I am on a much firmer footing than I have been at any
moment of the monstrous stretch of time since you first—and more
closely and vividly than any one else—saw me taken ill; and though I
have just lately shifted my date of sailing back to England from June 14
(for which I had taken my passage 6 months ago), to August 2d.,[44] I
have done so with certain confidence of being able (D.V.) to disem-
bark—or at least to embark—more or less completely well. I have
never, you will have observed, acknowledged the arrival of the abbre-
viated and green-covered "Outcry"—any more than I have done that
of the little report you addressed me of the evidently most massacred,
by the duffers of actors, "Saloon"[45] (which I took very kindly of you);
but these things are ancient history now; and with the hope of seeing

44. James disembarked at Liverpool on 8 August 1911, and reached Rye on the
next day.
45. See James's letter to Bosanquet, 4 August 1910: the "cut" copy of *The Outcry*
had reached him. *The Saloon* was grievously cut by the producer, Gertrude Kingston,
and misdirected as well as being incompetently acted in the Little Theatre in John
Adam St. in London.

you within so measurable a time I shall try then to make up all lapses of reference and recognition. One lapse indeed I mustn't any *more* preposterously wait (than I have already done), to repair. I beg you therefore to find herein my cheque for £10 in acknowledgment of the copy of The Outcry. I hope greatly that I shall not find you with your hands tied in respect to work—I mean with all your time mortgaged and disposed of. It is too soon for me to be sure of what I should like exactly to appeal to you for on my return—for it will then be a question for me of getting back to work myself for the first time since the autumn of 1909. I have been able to do nothing whatever here but devote myself to recovery. But on the other hand I have great plans and huge arrears. However if you *have* engaged yourself for the next ten years, so much the better for *you*! I don't even venture to assume absolutely that you are still at King's Cross Mansions[46]—so that I think I had better, for general safety's sake, address this to Miss Bradley's care at Rye. I feel that it will so reach you securely even if indirectly. I beg you to be very kindly remembered to her—and to Mrs. I hope you did get off to Florence—I hope above all you are in health and heart, and I am yours all faithfully

Henry James

105 PALL MALL, S.W.
October 27th, 1911

Dear Miss Bosanquet,

Oh if you *could* only have the real right thing to miraculously propose to me, you and Miss Bradley, when I see you on Tuesday at 4.30.[47] For you see, by this bolting in horror and loathing (but don't *repeat* those expressions!) from Rye for the winter, my situation suddenly becomes special and difficult; and largely through this, that having got back to work and to a very particular job,[48] the need of expressing myself, of putting it on, on the old Remingtonese terms, grows daily stronger within me. But I haven't a seat and temple for the Remington

---

46. Bosanquet was now lodged at 10 Lawrence St., Cheyne Walk, Chelsea, SW.

47. They met on Tuesday, 31 October 1911, at four-thirty.

48. Planned as a memorial to his brother William, the "job" turned into James's autobiography, the first volume of which, *A Small Boy and Others,* was published in New York and London in 1913.

and its priestess—*can't* have here at this club,[49] and on the other hand can't now organize a permanent or regular and continuous footing for the London winters, which means something unfurnished and taking *(wasting, now)* time and thought. I want a small, very cheap and very clean *furnished* flat or trio of rooms etc. (like those we talked of under the King's Cross delusion[50]—only better *and* with some, a very few, tables and chairs and fireplaces) that I could hire for 2 or 3—*3 or 4*— months to drive ahead my job in—the Remington priestess and I converging on it and meeting there morning by morning—and it being preferably nearer to her than to me; though near tubes and things for both of us! I must keep on *this* place for food and bed etc.—I have it by the year—till I really *have* something else, by the year—for winter purposes—to supersede it (Lamb House abides—for long summers). Your researches can have only been for the *unfurnished*—but look, *think, invent!* Two or three decent little tabled and chaired and lighted rooms would do. I catch a train till Monday, probably late. But on Tuesday! Yours ever,

Henry James

REFORM CLUB

PALL, S.W.

November 2, 1911

Dear Miss Bosanquet,

In the intoxication of my relief at having resolved the Remington problem on Tuesday,[51] I went yesterday and bought without more delay, 3 or 4 articles which I hope I shan't inconvenience you by asking you to take them gently in even if one or two—or all!—of them—have to be put into a corner of your own premises till the little rooms are ready.

---

49. The Reform Club would not allow him to have a female secretary in his rooms there.

50. James had investigated the possibility of setting up there: Bosanquet wrote earlier in this diary (25 December 1909), "Mr. James made many enquiries *re* the King's Cross Mansions in which Nellie and I had taken a flat. I think he quite entertains the idea of taking one himself—just to work in." See his letter to her of 14 May 1911, above.

51. Theodora had arranged for James to have two rooms adjoining her flat at 10 Lawrence St. in Chelsea, with his own bathroom and private entrance. The Reform Club was a ten-minute taxi ride from there.

These articles are—so far as I recollect—1st a wickerish kind of arm-
chair, the only thing of any size and which you will perhaps let abide in
your sitting-room till it can be shifted; 2nd a long piece—or strip—of
greenish felt to lie on the floor of the larger room (I had simply to *guess*
at length); and 3rd a set of washing-stand articles and waste paper bas-
ket. I shall send nothing more till the rooms are ready—when there may
be 2 or 3 more wants for me to supply. I find the question of the Letters
to be copied or dictated baffles *instant* solution, but shall have been able
to judge in 2 or 3 days. It is a bit complicated, and I may let it wait till I
begin to come. I shall rather like to begin with something that goes very
straight so as to get the easier back into harness. Yours very truly,

Henry James

ADDRESS: MISS BOSANQUET

10 LAWRENCE ST.

CHEYNE WALK

CHELSEA S.W.

REFORM CLUB

PALL MALL, S.W.

November 11th, 1911

Dear Miss Bosanquet,

Thanks for your note, which I found when I got home yesterday. I'm
afraid I didn't go into the question of the electric light (the place for
another lamp) as much as I meant to, but the attachment you showed
me seemed all right so far as that one goes, and we can judge of anything more later. As regards the plug just put in I mean that the position *by the window* is right, but the plug would certainly be best on the
wall. As for the coals question &c your suggestion has great force, and
our agreeing on the whole thing for 18/ a week suits me very well. I
shall be able to judge after a day or two as to anything I want further—
but what I really want most is just to get back to the dear old Remington tick. I hope to arrive with the ticker itself &c on Monday about
one; and I will bring a new ribbon which Wilton Rix told me it needs
(he looked it over the other day at L.H., coming all the way from Tonbridge for the purpose), and which I fear I must ask you to put on—
unless we send again to Tonbridge and to Wilton for the purpose.
Yours very truly,

Henry James

[Monday], 7 October 1912. I went up in the morning from Red Cottage to see how Mr. James was getting on after his recent attack of Shingles[52] and found him much better. . . . [Mrs. Prothero said,] "Well, Miss Bosanquet, Henry James is very fond of people when they are there, but I don't believe he cares a bit when they aren't. . . . I've often noticed that, friendly and charming as he is, he is really quite aloof from everyone. It's the artist in him."

Sunday, 20 October 1912. . . . But dreadful as was the tale he unfolded [of his brother William's last illness and death] his cheek took on a healthier tint while he did so, and by the end he was quite blooming. It's extraordinary what a lot of good effort does him, even the effort of slow conversational expression.

Sunday, 13 January [1913]. H.J. was able to struggle away from Rye about the 13th Dec. [1912] and he spent his time, till Saturday the 5th, at Garlant's Hotel in Suffolk Street. He didn't get on very well or fast there, and found it both expensive and depressing, but from the first night he slept at 21 Carlyle Mansions,[53] he began to gain strength and hope and he has done quite a decent amount of work this last week.

Friday, 24 October 1913. At three o'clock I went to keep an appointment with Mr. Pinker.[54] I had left some things (two short stories and the serial) with him after my last interview. That interview was mainly on Mr. James' account but I seized the opportunity to speak a few words for myself and to ask him to look at some of my stuff. Which he did and sent me a contract to sign, pledging myself not to traffic in any way but through him in stories and articles. A year's notice to terminate the agreement on either side. He to take a commission of 15% on stories and 10% on long things. . . . After all Miss Phelps foretold, by the Tarot cards when I was at Crediton, that I should succeed *certainly* "with the help of a man." May Mr. Pinker be he!

---

52. James was diagnosed as having shingles—*herpes zoster* or *zonalis*—on 4 October 1912. It persisted, with lapses, into the new year.
53. 21 Carlyle Mansions, Cheyne Walk, Chelsea: an L-shaped, five-bedroom flat on the north bank of the Thames, which James leased in December 1912 and occupied on the first weekend of 1913; it was quite near Bosanquet's flat in Lawrence St.
54. James Brand Pinker (1863–1922), James's literary agent since 1898.

Monday, 27 October 1913. . . . We left our rather shabby and dirty-looking flat for the cottage at Rye [i.e., Red Cottage, the Bradleys']. . . . I had forgotten how charming the cottage was. Or rather had never really realized it. Both Nellie and I. . . . Clara [Smith] was still here (working at Lamb House in my stead).

Friday, 2 October 1914. "Notes on Novelists" arrived at his flat this morning. He has very kindly given me a copy with one [of] his usual sorts of inscription. "Faithful fellow-worker" this time! . . . I believe Dent is actually publishing it on the 14th.[55] . . . I have *less* sense of the War here [London] than in Rye, especially in the mornings when I'm working. The River [Thames] is so exactly the same. . . . It was much more convincing to see the troopships from Camber.

Tuesday, 6 October 1914. [Mr. James dictated letters] on end till half past one. At which time I came home, buttered an egg and ate it to the accompaniment of 1/4 pint of stout (which I'm taking to try to get fat on!). . . . am going to be bed now (9:15).

Wednesday, 7 October 1914. Woke as usual at about half past seven, and waited till I heard the paper come. Then went down to make breakfast, which it is my habit to bring upstairs and feed on while I read the Times in bed.

Friday, 9 October 1914. . . . did a little work . . . and had supper on a tray. . . . now, (about 9:30) going off to bed.

Sunday, 1 November 1914. Mr. James started this morning on a long preliminary jawbation, to get himself worked up to the right pitch, about "The Sense of the Past," a tale projected some time ago, partly in response to advances made by some publisher friend of Rudyard Kipling's.[56] After it was started there was a hitch about it being pub-

---

55. *Notes on Novelists, with Some Other Notes* was published on the thirteenth in London by Dent and Sons, and on the fourteenth in New York by Scribner's Sons.

56. Rudyard Kipling (1865–1936), English poet and novelist. F. N. Doubleday, Kipling's American publisher, had discussed with James the possibility of doing another volume of ghost stories like "The Turn of the Screw." See James's note of 9 August 1910, *Complete Notebooks,* 189–91.

lished, and the author abandoned it. Now he thinks that it's sufficiently fantastic and divorced from present day conditions to be taken up and worked at. . . . Mr. James hasn't got the MS. as far as it went up here, so I'm to go to Rye on Tuesday to fetch it for him.

Wednesday, 4 November 1914. "The Sense of the Past" . . . quite what Mr. James wanted. . . . He began re-dictating it. At once there leaps up in me the old futile perverse objection to his *donnée,* or at least to an incidental one. He wants to give his young man a love affair, to be over before his psychic experience in London, and postulates a pretty young widow, herself quite cosmopolitan, in New York, who refuses to have anything to do with the man unless he makes a positive vow that he won't ever go to Europe. It seems to me a most absurd and unnecessary straining of the probabilities to introduce such an unnatural feature. No sufficient reason is even hinted at. However!

Thursday, 12 November 1914. I can't seem to *see* that Armiger situation [*The Sense of the Past*]. And yet I believe it has possibilities. But I know it's no good pegging on at it if it won't come. That always means there's something fundamentally wrong.

Wednesday, 13 January 1915. Mr. James has got away from letters a bit and is going on with his "Sense of the Past," which seems to me to embody such an essentially impossible idea, even "psychically," that I don't see how he *can,* with all his ingenuity, bring it to a really triumphant conclusion. But I'm coming more and more to the conviction that he doesn't really face and solve his problems, anyway not his problems of possibility, he trusts to his technique to obscure the fact that they are there at all.

Monday, 1 March 1915. I've had several days of holiday for a rather funny reason. Mr. James consented, for the first time in his life, to be "interviewed" the other day in connection with the American Motor-Ambulance Corps, by a representative of the New York Times. His consent, however, was only given on condition that he might see the Copy produced. That the young journalist brought round last Thursday. But H.J., finding that it wouldn't do at all from his point of view, has spent the last 4 days re-dictating the interview to the young man, who is, fortunately, a good typist. I should love to see the published result.[57] I think the idea of H.J. interviewing himself for four whole days is quite delightful!

Monday, 22 March 1915. Mr. James was writing letters this morning, one (such a dull one!) to Burgess [Noakes][58] who had written *him* an excellent letter. He can talk delightfully on paper whatever his limitations may be when it comes to actual speech. But I expect his usual limitations in speech aren't nearly as bad as Mr. James thinks. He naturally, like all the rest of us, judges people by their manner to *him,* and doesn't realize that it's very few people who can be their easy or natural selves in his company.

Friday, 24 September 1915. Found Mr. James in much better form and inclined to work. But before he began to "break ground" on a prefatory thing about Rupert Brooke, he discoursed at some length on his impressions of "Guy and Pauline," Compton Mackenzie's new novel.[59] He considers it above all things irresponsible . . . Guy, postulated as a poet, but not *shown* as such, not apparently moved by a single poetic thought.

Thursday, 2 December 1915. Kidd came over about breakfast-time to tell me that Mr. James seemed to have had a sort of stroke.[60] She had been in the dining-room at 8.30 and had heard him calling, and had gone in and found him on the floor. Naturally she thought it a heart-attack, but she soon discovered that his left leg had given way under him. She and Burgess got him back, with difficulty, into bed. I went

---

57. See Preston Lockwood, "Henry James's First Interview," *New York Times Magazine,* 21 March 1915.

58. Burgess Noakes (1884–1975) from Peasmarch, Sussex, James's valet and a bantamweight boxer, joined James's household in 1898. See Henry James, *Letters: 1895–1916,* vol. 4, ed. Edel (Harvard University Press, 1984), 737–40. Cf. p. 56, n. 51.

59. Edward Montague Compton "Monty" Mackenzie (1883–1972), son of Edward and Virginia (Bateman) Compton, who staged James's *The American* in 1890. James had praised his novel *Carnival* (1912). The new novel was just out.

60. James had been seriously suffering from heart trouble throughout the autumn of 1915. This was the first of a series of strokes. Minnie Kidd was James's housekeeper.

over immediately and saw Mr. James, who told me he had a stroke "in the most approved fashion." He had got out of bed, and when at the other side of the room he had collapsed. The most distressing thing, he said, was his sensation when he found himself fumbling with the wire of the electric lamp instead of the bell, fancying in a bewildered sort of way that they would connect. Then he tried shouting, and that brought Kidd. He was anxious to send a cable to Mr. Harry James, and while he spoke about it Dr. Des Voeux came.[61] So I left him, but saw the doctor afterwards, who said he had had a stroke, but quite a slight one, with no serious symptoms. I cabled at Mr. James's dictation "Had slight stroke this morning. No serious symptoms. Perfect care. No suffering. Wrote Pegg yesterday."[62] Then I went to 19 Thayer Street to try to get a male nurse for Mr. James. None available there, or at most of the other places the secretary there kindly tried. At last he heard of a man at a place near, in George Street, which I went to immediately. Not a prepossessing house, nor a prepossessing man, a tall, lanky, moustached creature, who was introduced as "Nurse Durham!" He didn't impress me very favourably, but I told him he would need great patience and all his intelligence, and the woman in charge assured me that he *was* patient and always brought back good reports, though her manner about him was a bit hesitating. However, he was the only thing to be got, so I told him to come down at once. Then went to the Aux. Stores to buy an extra bed and bedding and then back to the flat. Durham had not arrived, but came about 3. The servants reported him quiet, and Mr. James, when I saw him after tea, said he seemed "self-effacing but not callous." I didn't go back in the evening as Mr. James seemed better, but went in to 35 Rossetti Garden Mansions. Found Naomi[63] and Erica alone and had a quiet evening with them.

Friday, 3 December 1915. Found Miss Lily Norton[64] and Dr. Des Voeux talking together when I arrived in the morning. Dr. Des Voeux said

61. Des Voeux had been James's attending physician in London since 1914.
62. James's niece.
63. Naomi Royde Smith, an attractive literary hostess and a neighbor in the same block of flats as Bosanquet, was an editor in charge of the "Problems and Prizes Page" of the *Saturday Westminster Gazette;* she liked Bosanquet's writing, encouraged her, published her work in the *Gazette,* and became her friend.
64. Elizabeth "Lily" Gaskell Norton, daughter of James's old friend Charles Eliot Norton.

that Mr. James had had another stroke in the night and that the paralysis was much more complete. Kidd had had a cable from Mr. Harry James asking for full particulars from the doctor, and I took his cable to the Western Union office and added one from myself asking him to come if possible. Miss Norton most kind. I telegraphed to Mrs. Wharton too.[65] Also cabled to Mrs. Jones[66] as Kidd thought she would wish that done. Miss Norton said she would call at Brown Shipley's[67] and explain to the Manager the circumstances so that it might be possible for us to get some more money. When I got back from cabling found that Miss Sargent and Madame Ormond[68] had seen Mr. James and were arranging to spend the night sitting in the dining-room. Durham went out after lunch, promising to bring back another man, at the doctor's request. While he was away (he was gone 4 hours) Dr. Des Voeux brought Sir James Mackenzie[69] in to see Mr. James and they both thought him in a very grave condition. "Not absolutely hopeless" but not likely to recover unless he rallied fairly soon. At present practically unconscious. Dr. Des Voeux very much annoyed with Durham for leaving his patient for so long, as owing to his negligence Mr. James' head had been in a bad position and become congested. Miss Sargent was here when the doctors left Mr. James and heard their verdict, and asked if she and her sister mightn't spend the night here, to which they assented. Then when Sir J.M. had gone Dr. Des Voeux asked about Durham, and suggested that he had better go and get a couple of good trained female nurses to come. So I rang up a place he gave me the number of (a Miss Shebbeare's) and was lucky enough to get two nurses from there at once. Very nice women, especially the night nurse. Went into Mr. James's room for a little while he was having some tea, but he didn't notice me at all—was really very bad then, and later on Dr. Des Voeux, when he had been again, spoke most seri-

---

65. Two months earlier Bosanquet had promised Wharton (now back in France) to keep her informed of James's health etc.; see Diary B, entry for 6 October 1915.

66. Mary "Minnie" Cadwalader (Rawle) Jones (1850–1935), briefly married to Edith Wharton's brother Frederick, was a good friend of James.

67. James's international bankers, 123 Pall Mall, SW.

68. Emily Sargent (1857–1936) and Violet, Mme Francis Ormond (1870–1955), sisters of the American painter John Singer Sargent.

69. Eminent British heart specialist (1853–1925), whom James had first seen in February 1909.

ously of his condition. I had dined at Hornton Street and came in afterwards to find Madame Ormond already installed and Miss Sargent expected, and so I left her.

Saturday, 4 December 1915. Mr. James slightly better. I saw Miss Norton. She is so kind and nice and sensible. Took a cable reporting "distinct improvement" and adding a request for instructions in case of Mr. James' death before the arrival of his relatives. Then I went to Brown Shipley's and saw the Manager, Mr. Clark. He . . . wanted Mr. James to sign a cheque if he could. However, he advanced twenty-five pounds on my signature, thanks to Miss Norton having spoken preparatory words and given me an introductory card. Taxi'd back to Carlyle Mansions, and found Miss Allen[70] and Mrs. Prothero. Miss Allen . . . had only known by my note last night. . . . Mrs. Clifford . . . will come at a moment's notice. . . . Home to lunch . . . back to C[arlyle] M[ansions] for an hour in the afternoon. Arranged that the day nurse should sleep there . . . after [tea] . . . I went back to C.M., saw the doctor [Des Voeux]. . . . Went back for a few minutes at half past nine, no change, so home to bed.

Thurday, 9 December 1915. I went home to dinner and then came back and began reading the proofs for the preface to Rupert Brooke's "Letters from America"[71] which had just arrived . . . Home to bed, very tired.

Tuesday, 14 December 1915. Went across at nine. Rang up Mrs. James at Garlant's [Hotel]. . . . Mrs. Clifford[72] came in the afternoon. Told her about the objection taken by Mr. Spender[73] about the Westminster Gazette in the Preface to Rupert Brooke's "Letter from America."

---

70. Elizabeth Jessie Jane Allen (1845–1918), descendant of the Earl of Jersey and a friend of James's since 1899; because of her generosity to him and her dedication to benevolence and self-sacrificing behavior he nicknamed her "Goody"—after Little Goody Two Shoes.
71. The young English poet (1887–1915). James's last piece of professional writing was a preface for *Letters from America* (1916). Several of these *Letters* had prior publication in the *Westminster Gazette*.
72. Lucy, Mrs. W. K. Clifford (d. 1929), English novelist and playwright, one of James's oldest London friends.
73. Spender represented the *Gazette* in its threatened suit over James's comments in the preface, which expressed tart dismay that "a periodical which might have had as

Showed her Eddie Marsh's[74] letter, and told her about what I'd done yesterday, which I will make a parenthesis for here. (Monday morning. I went out at 11.30 . . . to Pinker's where I talked to him about H.J.'s health and we agreed he ought to be got to leave his literary baggage in the hands of Mrs. Wharton rather than run any risk of its falling into Harry James'. . . .)

Wednesday, 15 December 1915. Spent most of the afternoon excising and altering the libelous passages in the Rupert Brooke preface, and when I showed the results to Mrs. James was rewarded by her saying that "Henry would never know he hadn't written it himself." I do think it's quite a neat job—much better than what Mr. Eddy Marsh suggested himself.

Thursday, 16 December 1915. . . . Here I found two surprises. One a cake, left by the inaudible Miss Allen, as a kind little token; the other, from Macmillans, an "author's copy" of Mrs. Wharton's new book, "Fighting France."[75] . . . a very pretty little mark of gratitude for letters and telegrams received! Went back to Carlyle Mansions at 3 o'clock, but it really wasn't worth my while. Mrs. James won't use the drawing-room, as I'd intended her to, and doesn't have a fire in it, so that everyone who comes is ushered into the dining-room and stops both our occupations. And if she's going to see everybody there's no sense in my just being there as an extra wheel. Today Lady Bryce and Mrs. Page and Madame Ormond and Mrs. Hunter[76] all just over-

---

much more of him as it wanted should have wanted so moderate a quantity" ("Redictated Version of Preface to Rupert Brooke's 'Letters from America,'" p. 34, Houghton Library microfilm).

74. Edward Marsh (1872–1953), secretary to Winston Churchill and then attached to the office of Prime Minister Herbert Henry Asquith, was Brooke's friend and literary executor; Marsh's letter requested that Bosanquet amend the potentially libelous passage. See "The Handprinted Hogarth Essay," note 6.

75. *Fighting France, from Dunkerque to Belfort* (Scribner, 1915), an account of her experiences very near the actual western front.

76. Lady Bryce, wife of James, Viscount Bryce, who would bring to Henry James the insignia of the Order of Merit from King George V in January 1916; Mrs. Page, wife of the American ambassador to England, Walter Hines Page; Mary, Mrs. Charles Hunter (1857–1933), hostess at her substantial country house Hill Hall in Epping Forest to James and friends.

lapped each other, and though I wouldn't willingly have missed hearing Mrs. James' indignant repudiation of Mrs. Wharton and all her works (due to her shocked feelings when she read "The Reef" [1912]), except for that there was nothing at all worth being there for. And I had to scramble in my letters after the visitors had gone. A horrid arrangement. I must see if I can't have the typewriter in the other room even without a fire.

Saturday, 18 December [1915]. I showed Mr. Marsh the alterations I'd made [to the Rupert Brooke preface], and he approved and took off the proofs himself to give Frank Sidgwick.[77]

Wednesday, 29 December 1915. Went back to Carlyle Mansions [after luncheon], where I had a heart-to-heart with Mrs. James, who was kindness itself in regard to my position—says my salary is to be paid till March (which relieves me of all financial worries) and that I'm just to forge on ahead with my own literary work—such as it is! . . . We talked too of his disposition of his unfinished works—I told what he told me the morning after his stroke, and she quite understood the force of it all. Asked if I knew whether he had left the arrangement of his letters to Harry—which I didn't know at all. She said he was so frightfully busy—he hadn't even time to arrange his Father's letters yet,[78] though he has been dead five years. So certainly he can't do his uncle's. She almost hinted that I might perhaps be useful.

Saturday, 1 January 1916. A day of good omens! First the post brought me a letter from Pinker with an offer from Constable's for the Letters[79]—evidently the first publisher he tried so that is most encouraging. Then I saw in the Telegraph that Mr. James was in the list of New

77. Partner in the publishing firm Sidgwick & Jackson, Ltd., which published Brooke's *Letters from America* in England (1916); Scribner was the American publisher (1916).

78. Harry finally edited *The Letters of William James* in 2 vols. (Boston: Atlantic Monthly Press, 1920).

79. The epistolary novel *Spectators* that she had written in collaboration with her friend Clara Smith was duly published by Constable in May 1916. Their royalty was 15%: see end of entry for 15 January 1916 in this diary.

Year honours, with the Order of Merit.[80] So hustled across and was greeted by the news that he was much more himself and had been enormously pleased by the news. He had told Kidd to "turn off the light so as to spare my blushes," . . . he didn't speak when I congratulated him, but waggled a friendly hand at me.

Monday, 3 January 1916. I went back to C.M. afterwards [after tea]. . . . There was a telephone message from Sir Harry Legge wanting to know when he could see Mr. Henry James to deliver a message from the King, which Mrs. James is taking very little notice of.

Saturday, 8 January 1916. Got to C.M. when the doctor was there, and heard his report and a discussion about purgatives between him and Mrs. James. Received a very straight impression (from a piece of Peggy's writing left very much exposed) that I've given them the impression of being "above myself" and have enjoyed managing things in a heartless sort of way while the faithful servants have slaved to the breaking-point. Not very pleasant but no doubt excellent medicine for the soul. And I daresay it's largely true. I *have* probably been rather over-pleased by the kind way all Mr. James' friends have treated me, and have no doubt regarded it partly as an opportunity for myself! But heaven knows I was anxious enough for one of them to be over and managing things long ago. It was none of my wish to be alone with the household as at the recent catastrophe!

There was no work to do, so I came home again. Spent hours of the day copying out and slightly enlarging my diary for those first 12 days of Mr. James' illness. Mrs. James had asked me to do that for Peggy's benefit. Anyway, good or ill, the whole thing is on record, and though lots of people would have done better some might have done worse.

Nellie and I went to tea with Naomi [Royde Smith]—and discussed the dinner-club, and other things. Nothing very inspiring. Came back and finished copying diary pages. Even so I've left out the bit about Edmund Gosse. How I read his note to H.J., who said I was to "tell Gosse that my powers of recuperation are very great and that I'm making progress toward recovery without withdrawal."

---

80. The highest honor England could bestow on a civilian.

Sunday, 9 January 1916. Mrs. James gave me a letter from Lord Stanfordham to answer written on Dec. 28th to announce the coming of O[rder of] M[erit] and full of messages from the King. It needed an immediate reply!

Saturday, 15 January 1916. . . . called at C.M. and had a few uncomfortable moments with Mrs. James and Peggy. I was foolish enough to ask if Mrs. James would like me to write to Mr. Pinker "about the contract with Nelson's for the cheap edition of 'Roderick Hudson.' "[81] To ask, I explained, whether it wouldn't be a good plan for her to use her power of attorney to sign it. Mrs. James immediately said, "What in the world has Mr. Nelson to do with it [etc.] . . . ?" That bewildered me to a state of absolute blankness and I could only apologise and say that I'd meant to say "Pinker." "I'll see Mr. Pinker myself if necessary," Mrs. James said. Then she went on, "I saw that thing in the pigeon-hole. If I'd known of it ten days ago we could have gotten Henry's signature." That did upset me, because till the Power of Attorney had been agreed upon there had been absolutely no question of asking Mr. James to sign any business document, and when I'd asked if I should speak to him of it, not as a matter for a signature but just as a pleasant little literary fact, the doctor had suggested that it would be better not to discuss any business affairs at all. So I had simply told Pinker he was too ill to deal with it at all. However, Mrs. James was so huffed and frightened me so badly that I simply turned tail and fled—it would have been a funny sight for anyone who had an eye for the humorous. The presumptuous secretary being put in her place and slinking out of the presence of righteousness. ·

Came back and wrote letters—one to Mrs. Wharton. Read to Nellie a bit after lunch. She sat up for tea and afterwards dressed in honour of Clara who came to dinner and was very pleasant. Just as I was letting her out I found two things in the letter-box. One a card from Nora . . . ; the other Constable's contract for C[lara] and to me to sign, which we did with great joy. He has got us 15% royalty, which seems to me extraordinarily good for a first book by two unknown people.

81. With the permission of his English publisher, Macmillan, James had given his novel *The American* (vol. 2 of the New York Edition of his *Novels and Tales*) to Nelson and Sons for their series of cheap editions in 1913. Nelson wanted to add his novel *Roderick Hudson* (vol. 1 of the *Novels and Tales*) to the series.

Monday, 31 January 1916. Peggy James came round in the morning
. . . inviting us both to tea. . . . Mr. Harry James . . . nearly white-
haired, but still black-moustached. He has a tremendous chin—the
most obstinate-looking jaw. But he was pleasant enough. Asked me to
go through his uncle's typescripts—the unfinished novels, etc.—and
made lists of them for himself and Pinker. It was a relief to hear something I *could* do.

Monday, 28 February 1916. Went to enquire at C.M., and met Miss
Sargent in the hall. She told me Mr. James had died about three quarters of an hour before (a little before seven [p.m.] in that case, for I
saw her about half-past) quite painlessly and peacefully, without ever
regaining consciousness. He just gave three sighs, Mrs. James told her,
and went. I shocked her a little for expressing thankfulness for this
end, but she agreed at last that if he couldn't really recover it was
much the best thing after all. Didn't go up . . . though I sent a note to
Mrs. James asking her to send for me if there was anything I could do.
Sent a wire to Mrs. Wharton.

Wednesday, 1 March 1916. A good deal of Guild business and other
items to attend to all the morning. Went over to Carlyle Mansions in
the afternoon, where I found Peggy alone, very sad. She showed me
various newspaper cuttings, one odiously vulgar exhibition of Violet
Hunt's,[82] from the Daily Mail. It appears that there is a question of an
Abbey funeral—Mrs. Prothero and Mr. Bailey Saunders and Mrs.
Clifford are trying to arrange it. The dean isn't very willing, but says
it *could* be done. In the meantime 'it's more dignified,' as Peggy said,
for them to go on with the arrangements for the service here [in
Chelsea]. She asked me if I wouldn't like to see "the body," which, she
said, would be ready later on in the day. They had been taking a cast
of the face. So I came away then, but went back later, when Kidd took
me into the drawing-room, where he lies, already in his coffin, covered with a black pall, with a white square over the face, which she
folded back. One couldn't see anything but the actual face, for it was

82. Violet Hunt (1866–1942), English novelist, daughter of the painter Alfred
Hunt, sometime mistress of Ford Madox (Hueffer) Ford; James had known her
since her childhood.

bound round with a bandage. It looked very fine—a great work of art in ivory wax. Perfectly peaceful, but entirely *dissociated* from everything that was his personality. I quite understood what Mrs. James meant by speaking about the great feeling of tenderness one had for the dead body that is left behind. One feels that the spirit that inhabited it isn't there to care for it any longer and it would be the most impossible breach of trust not to surround it with care and reverence.

Went home and spent the evening reading the proofs [of the *Spectators* novel]. My part of the book strikes me as dreadfully bad except in a few patches. Clara's is all much better—which is just as well.

Friday, 3 March 1916. A pouring wet day for the funeral, of course. Mrs. James sent me a very kind note, asking if I wouldn't like to go see him just once more. . . . Mrs. James told me that George [Gammon, gardener at Lamb House] . . . had come up from Rye, . . . had seen his dead master. . . . She had a letter from the Dean of Westminster, explaining that a memorial service wasn't possible . . . Mrs. James had written him a reply—very nice and dignified, which she showed me and invited my assistance with the last sentence of. It was something to be able to help even in that way! She also asked me to go early to the church [Chelsea Old Church] and see that the wreaths were properly placed. Several people who have seen the dead face are struck with its likeness to Napoleon, which is certainly great, though she herself thinks it more like the head of Goethe. I went round to the church a little before half-past one, and found people beginning to arrive but the door not open. In a few minutes a troop of small choir boys came too, and had to wait outside. I fled back to C.M. to see if they knew where the verger was, but they didn't, so I was going to send a boy to the Rectory; but by the time I got back the verger had arrived and people were being let in. Mrs. Clifford and the Ranee of Sarawak[83] had been sitting quite comfortably in the Ranee's car, but other people had been getting quite wet. Mr. Bailey Saunders, who saw me standing about, waiting for the wreaths, mistook me for Peggy, and asked

---

83. Margaret Brooke, née Windt (1849–1936), in 1869 married her much older second cousin, Sir Charles Brooke, who succeeded his father as Rajah of Sarawak in northeast Borneo; Lady Margaret thus became Ranee. She was an old friend of James's.

if "my mother" was coming. Then he waited about too to assist with
the wreaths. The church had pretty well filled up by the time they
came—people poured in, and left their distinguished names with the
press at the door. Mr. Gosse, who was looking about for a seat,
wasn't at all pleased when I suggested that he should go to the side.
"But I came *early,*" he said, and he had evidently expected a reserved
place in the front row. Mr. Bailey Saunders and I got into a pew with
poor little swollen-eyed Miss Allen, just behind the one where the
Jameses were to sit.

By that time the church was full—much fuller than I imagine it can
be at all used to. It's full of mellow old tone, and if the organ had been
better and the choir more effective it would have been quite a good
place for the funeral service. The coffin was carried in and placed in
the chancel, which isn't at all raised, and the choir sang the opening
verses of the service. Mrs. James, Peggy, Mr. and Miss Sargent and
Madame Ormond, came in to occupy the front pew; and the servants
sat the other side. Dr. Des Voeux came into our pew. Mrs. Prothero,
who had come with that party, wandered away by herself to find a seat
on the far right. So the service began, and though the choir wasn't up
to much, it didn't go badly. Anyhow it was perfectly simple. Mr.
Bailey Saunders insisted on going to Golders Green afterwards [for the
cremation], though Mrs. James quite begged him not to. Still, I think
there was something to be said for a man being there, and I'm very
glad Miss Sargent and Madame Ormond were going with them. After
the service was over, the coffin carried out and taken off by motor to
Golders Green, followed by the Jameses and Sargents in a car, the rest
of us began to go out. I waited till they had all gone, and saw Ellen
Terry, being guided down the steps and into a car, and plenty of other
people who were no doubt celebrated but whose face I didn't know.
Mrs. Belloc-Lowndes[84] spoke to me most kindly. Afterwards I found
the Press (two of it) examining the names on the wreaths and little
Miss Allen searching the church for a spare copy of the scripture
paper. The pressmen said "There aren't many at all, are there?" not
recalling the "No flowers, by request" intimation.

Took Miss Allen up the street to a bus—she still mournful because

---

84. Marie Belloc-Lowndes (1868–1947), wife of F. S. A. Lowndes of the *Times* of
London and sister of the writer Hilaire Belloc, was herself a novelist.

the Jameses hadn't let her see him before he died—and then came home. Clara came in to tea and proof-reading.

· *Wednesday, 3 May 1916.* An awful gap here of over a month! That's due to my having been busy copying H.J.'s unfinished works all the time—"The Ivory Tower" and "The Middle Years."[85] The latter would have been a most remarkable and characteristic gallery of Victorian portraits, quite one of the most arresting ever exhibited. Oh, if only he had finished it instead of taking up "The Sense of the Past."[86] One can be grateful, however, that he did Tennyson and George Eliot and did them beautifully!

Mrs. James and Peggy away for Easter and 10 days after. I had the pleasure of a visit from Mr. Percy Lubbock[87] on the Sunday before Easter. He had written that he wanted to "talk about H.J." and he came to tea and talked a lot afterwards. He wanted really to discuss the question of what's to be done about the editing of the private letters etc., and joined me in a regret that Mrs. Wharton hadn't been left in charge. He feels it's awfully difficult to offer advice to people like the Jameses, and yet they do need some very badly! He's so full of sensitive feeling himself that he can't go boldly trampling in their reserves, as Mr. Pearsall Smith[88] more easily can. He came to tea on the previous Friday to meet with Mrs. J. and Peggy and I heard him offering them advice by the gallon. However, after our own talk, Mr. Lubbock went on to Carlyle Mansions.

I had of course thought of him as a possible and very good person to undertake the task of editing, but hadn't said anything to his face, partly from nervousness, in fact chiefly. But I heard later on in the

---

85. *The Ivory Tower* is one of two novels James left incomplete at his death. *The Middle Years* is the third volume of his autobiography, published in London and New York in 1917.

86. The other novel left incomplete at his death. He had begun work on the idea again in 1914, sent Bosanquet down to Rye at the beginning of November to recover the abandoned manuscript, and resumed dictating it to her. (See *Complete Notebooks,* especially p. 502.) It was subsequently added, with *The Ivory Tower,* to the New York Edition.

87. Lubbock (1879–1966), British critic and biographer, edited *The Letters of Henry James,* 2 vols. (1920).

88. Logan Pearsall Smith (1865–1946), American essayist and linguist.

week from Mrs. Wharton that Mr. Gosse had written her. This is what she said. "I hope so much to hear that Mr. Lubbock is to be asked to edit Mr. James's letters and to write about him. As Mr. Gosse wrote to me the other day, no one else is so well-fitted to do it, in fact I know of no one else who *could* do it, and I am so eager to hear that he has been asked to take entire charge."

I heard from Mr. Lubbock a day or two later, to say nothing was at all settled about the letters, but his name had been suggested to Mrs. James. "But I doubt," he delightfully said, "if they will be able to gather themselves up to do very much until they hear from Harry, and all depends on him giving them some positive directions—any word of his will be law, of course. . . . But in talking to them one seems (to you I will say it!) to move in such a cloud of fine discretions and hesitations and precautions that it is difficult altogether to know where one is."

So on the Sunday after Easter I went to call on Mrs. Clifford to see what her idea was. It isn't necessary to say that it was altogether for Mr. Lubbock. She told me, however, that Mr. Pearsall Smith has put forward Desmond MacCarthy[89] as a candidate. I don't think that a very sound suggestion, because, though he couldn't help doing something interesting, he wouldn't be able to see things from Mr. James' own standpoint with the sympathetic understanding P.L. would bring to his task.

. . . talk to Mrs. P[rothero] about the Letters. She had only heard . . . having tea with Mrs. James and Mrs. Clifford . . . that they were more or less collecting letters. So I told her all about how iniquitous it would be if Harry James edited them, and how fitting it was that Percy Lubbock should, and she entirely agreed, and so did her husband when he came in.

Thursday, 4 May 1916. I went round early to Carlyle Mansions to ask Mrs. James if Pinker was to value the copy of the Preliminary Statement to the Ivory Tower[90] as well as the work itself, and she agreed that he had better see it. Had a blessed moment at the door with Peggy who "gathered herself up" to the point of actually asking if I had any

---

89. Charles Otto Desmond MacCarthy (1877–1952), gifted literary critic and a member of the Bloomsbury group, met James in 1901.
90. See *Complete Notebooks,* 466–501.

suggestion to make as to the best person to edit the letters. Luckily too her own judgment is all in favour of Mr. Lubbock, and she said she should "write to Harry again" about him.

Then I hurried off to Arundel Street, bearing the typescripts with me, and gave them to Mr. Pinker. Had a most interesting talk with him. He has no more opinion of Mrs. James than Nellie! He assured me that he didn't in the least believe a statement she had made him to the effect that the family had for years contributed to the upkeep of Lamb House. She had brought that subject up in connection with Mrs. Wharton, as to whom she expressed herself very freely, and her iniquity in associating herself with the squashed thousand pound gift which was to have been for his seventieth birthday.[91] He says the copyrights are all left to Mrs. James and Lamb House to Harry. He thoroughly approved of Percy Lubbock (who is to see him tomorrow) since Mrs. Wharton is "impossible." He has been convinced by his recent communications with Scribners' that his guess as to Mrs. Wharton having subsidized the Scribner novel contract was quite correct,[92] and thinks that if Mrs. James hears that Scribners don't want to have the part payment already made liquidated she won't in the least want to liquidate it and in that case will be unwittingly benefiting to a pretty good tune from the gift of her hated enemy. Pinker's theory is that Mrs. James will always be accessible to the argument of pecuniary profit. . . . As an example of her utter lack of literary understanding—she told Pinker that in her opinion "The Middle Years" wasn't worth publishing!

---

91. In England a plan directed by Percy Lubbock, Edmund Gosse, and the young novelist Hugh Walpole (1884–1941) to collect modest sums (10 shillings to £5) from a number of contributors led to purchase of a silver gilt porringer—a "golden bowl"—for James on his seventieth birthday. Mrs. Wharton planned a gift for James from American contributors, "not less than $5,000" (or £1,000; she wanted to enable him to purchase an automobile for himself). When James learned of the plan, he insisted on *it* being stopped. In compensation, James added the names of Wharton and Walter Berry to the list of donors of the English gift when he expressed his thanks.

92. In 1912, Mrs. Wharton persuaded Charles Scribner to offer James an advance of $8,000 for "an important American novel," $4,000 on his beginning work on it and $4,000 on completion; the money to be diverted from her royalties from Scribner. On receipt of the advance James resumed work on the incomplete *The Ivory Tower* for a short time. He never learned of the true source of the $4,000.

Wednesday, 23 August [1916]. Worked in the morning. Read "The Figure in the Carpet" to Nellie in the afternoon. Mrs. Colley called to return Jacob Stahl and to borrow the next two volumes.

Met P. Lubbock at Hyde Park Hotel grill room, 8.15 and we had an excellent dinner, with champagne! Had a long and most interesting talk about H.J. and the Letters, which have been put entirely into his hands,[93] with a request that he will go to Mr. Gosse for any advice he needs. That, as Mr. Gosse himself quite sees, is to keep him from coming under the "influence" of Mrs. Wharton. Mrs. James, apparently, definitely said to him that it would be better to have the letters copied by a stranger than by me! Peggy, he says, didn't agree. However, he seems inclined to put a certain amount of work in my hands. We walked down Sloane Street afterwards and parted at Sloane Square, he saying he would let me know definitely after that. Have a general feeling I was very indiscreet and let myself go far too much. Much too excited to sleep, at any rate for some hours. Sickening to have such a feeble set of nerves!

Wednesday, 11 October 1916. I worked, copying H.J.'s letters, in morning.

Thursday, 12 October 1916. Copied the packet of 1901 letters, from Lamb House. The most interesting dealing with Henley's article on Stevenson.[94]

Sunday, 15 October 1916. I copied Letters—they seem to me less interesting as they go on—so largely taken up with explanations about the "complications" which have prevented their being written before.

---

93. Bosanquet was thoroughly involved in the preparation of Lubbock's edition of *The Letters of Henry James,* as subsequent diary entries indicate.

94. William Ernest Henley (1849–1902), English poet, critic, editor, and playwright, published in the *Pall Mall Magazine* (Christmas no. 1901) a harsh review of *The Life of Robert Louis Stevenson* (1901) by Graham Balfour (1858–1929) charging that Balfour treated his subject too generously. Henley and the Scottish novelist Stevenson (1850–94) had once been friends and collaborated on four plays in the 1880s. The denigration of Stevenson's character in the review shocked the British public, and James, who had been a dear friend of Stevenson for over thirty years.

Nellie did some pen and ink work, which looks like quite the sort of thing they want for illustrating the book.

In the afternoon we walked about Cheyne Walk and Royal Hospital Road—parted at the Hospital, where N. turned off though the grounds, and I went to Sloane Square and took train for Paddington to call on Mrs. Clifford. The maid said she wasn't "at home" on Sundays till November, but was seeing callers, and I found the drawing-room already occupied by Ezra Pound[95] and a slow-speaking, vacant-eyed grey-moustached man, as well as Mrs. C and her daughter, at last more or less restored to health. Mrs. C. enquired at once if I'd heard anything from the Jameses, and when I said I'd only had a letter from Kidd, exclaimed that that was all anyone had! Mrs. Prothero's maid heard from Kidd, but nobody has had a line from either Peggy or Mrs. James, much to their surprise and rather to their annoyance.

Rather bored by the conversation of the elderly Mr. Morrison, as I gathered his name to be. Ezra Pound, on the other hand, sunk into his arm-chair and his brown velvet coat, would have been extremely interesting and was very witty, only one can't hear more than half the creature says in his languid manner. His account of a tea-party at Marie Corelli's[96] was full of good things, of which I caught only detached fragments of embroidery. Mrs. John Collier came in afterwards and the man Morrison, and afterwards E.P. left. Mrs. Clifford most kind and friendly, though afflicted by a horrid cold.

---

95. American expatriate poet (1885–1972).
96. The pen name of Mary Mackay (1855–1924), author of popular romances.

Diary B

🐎 Theodora Bosanquet's Literary Taste and
Affiliations (WITH ONE EXCERPT FROM A LETTER)

Tuesday, 14 April [1908]. I went to iron ties with Nellie's attractive little iron before tea . . . went again after supper and read Nellie 2 really very clever satirical stories of Mrs. Wharton's—"The Descent of Man" and "Expiation."[1] I do enjoy the light sure touch she employs.

Saturday, 1 November [1908]. Mr. James recommenced work, after a week's break . . . Mrs. Wharton is staying with him,[2] but I didn't see her—only heard the snorting of her motor car, in which she went off to Ashford to luncheon.

Monday, 16 November [1908]. Introduced to Mrs. Wharton—fairish-bright hazel eyes, brown much-wrinkled skin—looks tired—quite pleasant. I was an awkward fool as usual.

Monday, 14 December [1908]. A day of some interest—and much rain! I struggled, in the afternoon, up to the Waterlows[3] to tea—and there

---

1. Wharton's "The Descent of Man" (1904) and "Expiation" (1903) are tales from her collection *The Descent of Man* (Scribner, 1904).
2. Wharton was in England for the last eight weeks of 1908 and much of the time with James—in London, at Howard Sturgis's Queen's Acre, at Lamb House, and elsewhere.
3. Sydney Philip Perigal Waterlow (1878–1944), sometime British ambassador to Greece, and a neighbor of James's in Rye; his wife, Alice, was daughter of Sir Frederick and Lady Pollock. Sir Frederick was formerly Corpus Professor of Jurisprudence at Oxford.

met Mr. E. M. Forster,[4] who wrote "A Room with a View," etc.—an
extraordinarily good book. He looks as young and clever as possible,
and has a charming unassuming manner. They had another visitor, a
Manchester lady, whose name I didn't catch—very keen on women's
suffrage. We talked that and about Mr. James' novels mostly. Mr.
Waterlow lent me Mr. Lowes Dickinson's last book—"Justice and
Liberty"[5] which I shall enjoy.

Sunday, 13 January 1913. . . . before I get on to the present I want to
write down what I can remember of his remarks about Mrs. Wharton's "The Reef."[6] It's such a good example, it seems to me, of his
blind affection for an imitation of his own manner, for I don't really
think Mrs. W. is so good in this rather tired book, with its overdone
coincidences and its occasional false notes in the psychology (as, e.g.
Anna's writing the same facts *twice* to Darrow and her abandonment
that last night at Givre), as in the wonderful little masterpiece Ethan
Frome [1911]. But H.J. says that "not only is it the best thing Mrs. W.
has ever done, but it's the finest thing *any* woman has ever done!" And
in writing to her he ventured to compare it with her others (obviously
Ethan Frome), telling her how glad he was she had shaken herself free
from the suggestions of the influence of George Eliot!! Mrs. Wharton
herself suggests that she is disappointed in it, calls it "hastily written,"
and was worried by losing the proofs for a month, or rather the proofs
being lost for a month before they reached her.

Thursday, 22 October 1913. . . . the Thursday evening gathering at Adair
House and found Walter de la Mare, Agnes Conway,[7] Miss Goodman,
the colourless little Miss McCrae and—last but chief—Mr. and Mrs.

---

4. Edward Morgan Forster (1879–1970), British writer; *A Room with a View* (1908)
is his third novel.
5. Lowes Dickinson became a close friend of E. M. Forster, who published a biography of him in 1934.
6. Novel published in 1912. See the letter of 4 and 9 December 1912 to Wharton,
which James dictated to Bosanquet, *Henry James and Edith Wharton, Letters
1900–1915,* ed. Lyall H. Powers (New York: Scribner, 1990), 237–42.
7. Daughter of Sir Martin and Lady Conway of Allington Castle, Maidstone, Kent,
friends of James. De la Mare (1873–1956), British poet and man of letters.

Blanco White[8] there. She is just exactly like Wells' description of her in Ann Veronica,[9] except that her mouth and chin aren't good and one doesn't get a pretty profile effect. But seen from across the room she is strikingly good looking, with her masses of the very blackest hair and her thin pale face and slightly (attractively) oblique eyes. . . . Naomi Royde Smith . . . sustained the burden of the entertainment.

Wednesday, 12 November 1913. Mrs. Humphry Ward's "Coryston Family" . . . seems awfully artificial, so *made*—! He [James] has had an interesting book of Aubrey Beardsley's "Last Letters" send him by the man (Raffalowitch or something like that)[10] to whom they are mostly written, and who was apparently the means of getting him into the fold of the Catholic church . . . Mr. James talked a good deal about the man R. and how he was converted from a fast and wild life to Roman Catholicism and now lives a godly existence in Edinburgh.

Tuesday, 17 March 1914. . . . a great "bust" today at the Poetry bookshop . . . the anniversary of its opening[11] . . . reading by Lascelles

8. Amber Reeves, a brilliant young woman (double first in the Moral Sciences tripos at Cambridge) and a beauty, in 1908 became the mistress of H. G. Wells; her pregnancy in April 1909 created a crisis solved by the agreeable young lawyer G. Rivers Blanco White (a Cambridge Fabian like Amber): he and Amber married in July 1909, and a daughter was born at the end of December.

9. This novel (1909) of Wells's is a thinly veiled autobiography: not only are Sidney and Beatrice Webb satirized in the characters Oscar and Altiora Bailey, but his affair with Amber Reeves is evident in the relationship of the science teacher at Capes and his student Ann Veronica Stanley (as Bosanquet obviously recognized). In his subsequent novel *The New Machiavelli* (1910) Wells again rehearses that affair in the relationship of the politician Richard Remington and the young Isabel Rivers.

10. *The Last Letters of Aubrey Beardsley, with an introductory note by the Reverend John Gray* (1904). Beardsley (1872–98) was an important British artist and illustrator. Marc-André Raffalovich (1864–1934), affluent Russian cosmopolitan, was baptized at the Church of the Jesuit Fathers in Mayfair on 3 February 1896; Father John Gray joined the Roman Catholic Church on 19 March 1890. Gray and Raffalovich, both intimately associated with Oscar Wilde, became lovers. Beardsley was received into the Roman church by Father David Bearne on 31 March 1897. The "godly existence" of Raffalovich needs some qualification: see James's letter to Hugh Walpole (whose father was Anglican bishop of Edinburgh) for information about "immorality on stone floors" involving Raffalovich. *Letters,* ed. Edel, 4:694–95.

11. The Poetry Bookshop in Devonshire St., London.

Abercrombie of "The End of the World."[12] I went to Henry New-
bolt's lecturette on XX Century poetry. . . . saw Edmund Gosse. . . .
Newbolt spoke . . . of seven of the younger poets as especially worth
observing: Walter de la Mare and Gordon Bottomley . . . James
Stephens and Ralph Hodgson . . . Rupert Brooke, who has closest
affinities with John Donne . . . W. Gibson[13] . . . and finally Lascelles
Abercrombie . . . like Milton . . . followed by his reading of his play
"The End of the World."

Thursday, 12 November 1914. I bought the latest Bain, "A Syrup of the
Bees," and "A Pastor's Wife" by the Countess von Arnim.[14]

Friday, 13 November 1914. Spent the evening reading to Nellie. "The
Pastor's Wife" is excellent for the purpose. More alive on every page
than anything else except Rose Macaulay.[15]

Thursday, 19 November 1914. I lose all critical faculty about Countess
von Arnim, just as I do about Rose Macaulay, though not so
absolutely. But I'd read *anything* either of them chose to write in the
sure and certain hope of finding flashes of insight and gems of wit as I
can't really trust any other writers for.

12. Abercrombie (1881–1938), British poet, critic, and playwright; the play was
published in *Four Short Plays* (1922).
13. Henry John Newbolt (1862–1938), British poet; Bottomley (1874–1948),
British poet and playwright, biographer of Abercrombie; Stephens (1882–1950),
British poet and prose-writer, author of the very popular fiction *The Crock of Gold*
(1912); Hodgson (1871–1962), British poet; Wilfrid Wilson Gibson (1878–1940),
British poet.
14. *A Syrup of the Bees* (1914) by Frederick William Bain (1863–1940). Australian-
born Mary Annette Beauchamp (1866–1941) married Graf Hennig August von
Arnim (1851–1910) in 1889, becoming the Gräfin or Countess von Arnim, and
published the very popular *In a German Garden* (1898) under the pseudonym "Elizabeth," which she used for most subsequent publications; her novel *The Pastor's Wife*
was published in 1914. She became Countess Russell in 1916 upon marriage to
Francis, Lord Russell (1865–1931), elder brother of Bertrand Russell.
15. Emilie Rose Macaulay (1881–1958), British novelist and poet, began publishing in the *Saturday Westminster Gazette* in 1905—shortly before Theodora Bosanquet
did—and was a close friend of Rupert Brooke. Early in 1914 she published her sev-
enth novel, *The Making of a Bigot,* and her first volume of poetry, *The Two Blind Countries* (Sidgwick & Jackson).

Wednesday, 2 December 1914. . . . joined Nora and Clara at the Kingsway for a performance of the Dynasts.[16] It was a little too much like potted history, but many of the scenes were awfully effective. . . . The Napoleon scenes were spoilt, I thought, by the interpreter of the part, Sydney Valentine. He looked (and seemed) so much more like a Joseph Chamberlain,[17] who was, after all, a very very great personality.

Monday, 13 September 1915. . . . at Truelove and Hanson's . . . bought a new half-crown of Hueffer's called "Between St. Denis and St. George,"[18] his account of the English, French and German civilizations and the ideals they are fighting for, etc. It's just as extraordinarily *readable* as Hueffer has an invariable knack of being. Even I, who find it terribly hard to concentrate on anything I'm reading, can't skim him. He does write so interestingly that one can't help attending! Here he is out to slay the Pacifists, and he has just the same *sort* of mind that they have—I mean Shaw[19] and the others—he is absolutely the right man to be pitted against them.

Wednesday, 6 October 1915. A thrilling day. I went to Mr. James at 11 . . . he wasn't feeling well and had just been telephoning Mrs. Wharton . . . She in her turn asked if he could lend me to her this morning for some work! . . . I was very untidy, so I hurried back and changed into respectable clothes and then made a rather flurried way to Brook Street (Buckland's Hotel), where I was conducted through Mrs. Wharton's private sitting-room to her bedroom, where I found her in a very elegant bed-jacket, pink, with a cap of ecru lace adorned, as far as I could make out, with fur (if it wasn't hair!) and very pretty brown hair showing under it. Her arms were very much displayed, coming

16. Thomas Hardy (1840–1928), British poet and novelist, published his "Epic-Drama of the War with Napoleon in Three Parts, Nineteen Acts, and One Hundred and Thirty Scenes" between 1903 and 1908 with Macmillan. It was never produced in its entirety, but several productions of selections from *The Dynasts* were staged; Bosanquet saw the substantial selection of scenes staged by Harley Granville Barker at the Kingsway Theatre in London.
17. Joseph Chamberlain (1836–1914), British statesman and father of Neville Chamberlain (1869–1940), prime minister (1937–40).
18. *Between St. Denis and St. George: A Sketch of Three Civilizations*, 1915.
19. George Bernard Shaw (1856–1950), Irish dramatist and critic.

from very beautiful frills of sleeve, and they were good arms, not either scraggy or too fleshy, but just the right plumpness and ending up in hands most beautifully manicured. She was a bit over-scented and her room was terribly hot, but that was quite necessary with such flimsy garments as she was wearing. She said she had a touch of influenza, but she didn't appear to have any of the symptoms. Her face is squarish, and her complexion browny-yellow and wrinkled finely. She has good eyes, and a strong mouth. We talked, naturally, mainly about Mr. James, for she said at once, "Of course, Miss Bosanquet, I didn't really want you to come here to write letters for me, but just so that we might have a quiet talk."[20] I was able to tell her a good many things she didn't know, such as that Mrs. William James and Peggy had so very much wanted to come over last winter and weren't allowed, and that Dr. Harrison[21] considered that it was real genuine angina and not the simulated sort. She is going to try very hard to persuade him to have an elderly, well-trained man-servant—but I very much doubt if she will find that a possible things to persuade him to. I suggested that Kidd might perhaps be provided with a remedy in case of a sudden heart attack, and she said she would ask Mrs. Jones to see about that. After we had discussed Mr. James very hard and long we had a little talk about the War. And Mrs. Wharton told me the inner story of the Grand-Duke Nicholas's[22] retirement to the Caucasus. He lost 90,000 men at Brest-Litovsk, and he was very intimately associated with the reactionary party who closed the Duma. She said they don't think in Paris that the advance will progress any further now, but their hopes were high last week. The English are admitted to have fought well! But the French have no opinion of our officers, except Sir John French's Chief of Staff.

I was rather unhappily conscious all the time we were talking that I wasn't as much charmed as I ought to be. I could *see* the charm and I couldn't feel it—and that was so disappointing. I'm afraid I must be getting dreadfully old and cold-hearted. But it's some consolation to be able to guess what it must be for other people. Because she so evi-

---

20. Wharton wanted Bosanquet's promise to keep her constantly informed about James's health: he had been plagued with heart trouble and would indeed experience another attack in mid-October.

21. A temporary substitute.

22. Russian general (1865–1929).

dently *depends* on fascinating people all about her, her whole effect makes one continually conscious of that. Unfortunately I feel too diffident to take up the literary conversational opportunities, and yet she did, surprisingly, offer some. At the end of the interview she spoke of her wish to see Mrs. Woods, who, she said, had sent her a most charming contribution for The Book of the Homeless.[23] So after I'd walked out into Brook Street, I made the best of my way to the Temple, hoping to catch Nellie and to deliver Mrs. Wharton's message to Mrs. Woods.

Friday, 22 October 1915. . . . a note from Clara and her copy of "The Research Magnificent"[24] for me to read—which I immediately began to do. I wonder whether I'm just dazzled by a meretricious glitter of pellucid style—or whether Wells really *is* (mentally) the wonder he is always striking me as being. This book is much better than "The Wife of Sir Isaac Mammon"—much more alive. And he does—yes, he certainly *does*—think further and above all *clearer* than most people. I wish his frankness and penetration could be allied, for a change, to a different sort of temperament. It's interesting and valuable to have all these human documents and these flashes and impressions of life as it seems to H. G. Wells—but that makes one long only the more for the equally vivid and sincere impressions of life as it shows itself to other people—and they aren't able to be sincere like that. Hueffer comes nearest in a thing like "The Good Soldier."[25] . . . and Rose Macaulay strikes me as being perfectly sincere—but her books haven't quite the same value as Wells' (I mean in that respect—in others they have much much more) just because her temperamental outlook is so sophisticated that heaps and heaps of very definite human complications must look like the merest dirty [linen?] to her . . . I suppose I'm rather *like* Wells in some ways.

23. Or *Le Livre des Sans-Foyers,* ed. Wharton, was a collection of original and unpublished contributions from Belgian, French, English, Italian, and American authors, painters, and composers to be sold to benefit the American Hotels for Refugees and the Children of Flanders Rescue Committee founded in Paris by Wharton, published by Scribner at the turn of 1915–16.

24. H. G. Wells's novels, *The Research Magnificent* (1915) and *The Wife of Sir Isaac Mammon* (1914).

25. London: John Lane, 1914.

Wednesday, 10 November 1915. . . . a Meeting with speeches by John Buchan and Stephen Graham at Sutherland House.[26] . . . I took the strongest dislike to John Buchan. I think I loathe academically distinguished men. I hated his manner and his too obvious oratorical art and even his matter, though it wasn't an uninteresting account of the warfare on the western front.

Thursday, 21 January 1916. Called at C[arlyle] M[ansions] about 11. . . . Had a very nice letter from Mrs. Wharton this morning suggesting that I should be her secretary. I don't think I shall—it's too alarming a prospect—but it was most awfully nice of her to make the offer.

53, RUE DE VARENNE

[PARIS]

17 January 1916

Dear Miss Bosanquet,

. . . I wonder if, later, there wd. be a chance of your coming to me as a secretary? There are three difficult conditions.

1. Living in Paris, where you wd. probably be lonely at times.
2. Speaking & writing French easily—do you?
3. Having to begin work at 9 A.M.—& having to do queer odds & ends of things for me—a muddle of charity, shopping & literature—! Perhaps you don't think the picture tempting. (The muddle of things is of course due to war time, & is *not* the habitual duty of my secretary!)

It would be very pleasant to have you undertake the task, if only for a few months; & perhaps we might arrive at some kind of compromise even if you haven't the habit of writing French. It *would,* of course, be necessary that you should speak it enough to get about, & to communicate with the natives. . . .

Yours very sincerely

E. Wharton

---

26. Buchan (1875–1940), Baron Tweedsmuir, Scottish historian and popular novelist (e.g., *The Thirty-Nine Steps,* 1915), governor general of Canada, 1935–40.

Sunday, 23 January 1916. Wrote declining Mrs. Wharton's offer on grounds of health, lack of French, and literary possibilities here—though goodness knows *they* probably won't amount to much.[27]

Tuesday, 28 March 1916. . . . bought one of Countess von Arnim's books, to add to the seven-penny collection of her. I hear that she has married Lord Russell and nobody can think why unless it's for more "copy." Anyway she writes so delightfully which ever of her books one picks up, that I hope she'll go on even if she has plenty of money now.

Wednesday, 29 March 1916. We sat and watched Miss Rebecca West[28] writing her letters in the smoking room, and very untidy her black hair looked. . . . Rebecca West is effective now on platform. . . . But, of course, *very* much vulgarized! Her disjointed remarks about reviewing (prefaced by a cheap allusion to the book she had just written about Henry James) was cleverish enough to keep one interested and all on the cheap side of goodness. She announced at one point that there was only one critic existing in England at the moment—Mr. Ford Maddox [*sic*] Hueffer. That was perhaps aimed at Violet Hunt, who was immediately in front of us—a lean, fair-haired creature, still good-looking in a hard sort of way.

Wednesday, 7 June 1916. I went off to take copies to Pinker, I had already left the originals in the flat [21 Carlyle Mansions] for Mrs. James. And took a sort of farewell wander round in its lonely, empty state.

Monday, 17 July 1916. . . . after the daily effort to lick an article on H.J.[29] into shape that simply won't be licked, I . . . went to see Mrs.

<hr />

27. For Wharton's response of 26 January 1916, see *James and Wharton Letters,* 391; see also Bosanquet's impressions noted for 6 October 1915, above, especially the last paragraph.
28. Cicily Isabel Fairfield (1892–1983), British novelist and journalist, adopted the *nom de plume* "Rebecca West" from the character in Ibsen's *Rosmersholm* (a role she played during her year with the Royal Academy of Dramatic Art); she began a ten-year affair with H. G. Wells in 1913, which produced a son in 1914, the writer Anthony West; her critical study *Henry James* appeared in 1916.
29. "Henry James," published in the *Fortnightly Review,* June 1917, reprinted in August 1917 in *The Living Age* (England) and *Bookman* (United States). See introduction to this volume.

Clifford . . . And after I'd been there a bit a strange-looking man came in whom I soon identified as Ezra Pound. I don't know how he'd look with his hair and clothes conforming more to the hair and clothes of other men, but as it is with thick fluffy brown hair growing back from a very straight line along his forehead and a little pointed moustache and beard and slightly aesthetic clothes—he certainly makes an effect. He speaks with a bit of an American drawl in the smallest voice that could possibly be audible. It often wasn't. Mrs. Clifford treated him quite kindly, and floundered about after him like a good-natured elephant trying to follow the movements of a flickering lizard. He spoke a little of Henry James, saying of his naturalisation that it was "America's intellectual death-warrant," and of the rottenness of America in general—a country he hasn't a shred of belief in. Then we asked him his opinion of Rebecca West (I've got her book on H.J. and find it very vigorous and interesting though not exactly final) and his opinion is that she's a young woman of great ability, with a great natural feeling for differences of style—she nearly always spots writers whether their work is signed or not, he says, and a flair for knowing what it *going to be* important.

Tuesday, 1 August 1916. The Jameses go back to American next week. Peggy came in to tea on Monday and carried off a very rough carbon copy I had made of the various preliminary statements. She talked of Rebecca West's little book on H.J. with great fury and scorn, but liked immensely Percy Lubbock's article in the Quarterly,[30] which we thought very sympathetic and understanding but a little indefinite and disconnected. Rebecca West is liable to very vulgar lapses and isn't at all fundamentally sympathetic, but there's something to be said for her vigorous style, and where she does admire she does it very wholeheartedly. She can't help being intelligent and something had rubbed off onto her, but she's too intent on holding up H.J.'s limitations to view to lay enough stress on his greatness. He went so much further than anyone else has ever been along his own line just *because* he spent all his time at the one business of receiving and analysing and apprais-

---

30. "Henry James," *Quarterly Review,* July 1916, 60–74.

ing and transmitting the impressions life showered on him. It's ridiculous to blame him for not appreciating the lessons of history or the rights of women.[31]

---

31. See section VIII, *Henry James at Work.* West's criticism of James in her 1916 *Henry James* is at points quite similar to Wells's in his vicious satire of James in *Boon, The Mind of the Race, The Wild Asses of the Devil and the Last Trump* (1915)—a lack of "ideas" and an opaque and complex style; but her sympathetic and intelligent appreciation of James is markedly beyond Wells's scope. It is ironic that, on the one hand, Bosanquet's private exasperation over James's complexity and verbosity (confided to her diaries) closely resembles West's (and thus to some extent Wells's) and, on the other, West's appreciation of James despite his having a mind "so fine that no idea could violate it" (as T. S. Eliot said) so closely resembles Bosanquet's appreciation of him. West objects to James's "late style" and attributes its quality to his habit of dictating—and the echo of Wells's attack is evident in this passage from the closing paragraphs of *Henry James:*

> . . . one perceives that the crystal bowl of Mr. James's art was not, as one had feared, broken. He had but gilded its clear sides with the gold of his genius for phrase-making, and now, instead of lifting it with a priest-like gesture to exhibit a noble subject, held it on his knees as a treasured piece of bric-à-brac and tossed into it, with an increasing carelessness, any sort of object—a jewel, a rose, a bit of string, a visiting-card—confident that the surrounding golden glow would lend it beauty. (115)

(In *Boon* Wells compares a James novel to an empty church: "And on the altar, very reverently placed, intensely there, is a dead kitten, an egg-shell, a bit of string.") Nevertheless, Rebecca West was capable of responding sensitively to James's talent: "For although he could not grasp a complicated abstraction, . . . an idea that could be understood only by a synthesis of many references, he could dive down serenely, like a practiced diver going under the sea for pearls, into the twilit depths of the heart to seize its secrets" (99).

Diary C

🐎 Theodora Bosanquet and Psychic Phenomena

(WITH AN EXCERPT FROM A CONTEMPORARY DIARY)

Wednesday, 1 January 1908. Mr. James wrote letters—to a nephew "Alexander"—and to "William and Letitia"[1]—and, dear man, explained all about the people he was writing to. I *do* enjoy his letter-writing mornings. I gather that Professor [William] James is coming over to lecture at Oxford in the spring[2]—*oh* that I might see him. He'll come here—but oh, shall *I*?

Friday, 6 March 1908. Preface continued, and typed 2.30–4.30 in afternoon too—then to tea at Mrs. Leo Vidler's[3] where met Miss Bradley's friend Miss M. Vidler—rather interesting—didn't get her on Psychical matters though which are, I believe, her real topic.

Saturday, 18 [July 1908]. Introduced to Professor W. James!

Tuesday, 21 July [1908]. Found Professor James in the garden room where I went in and he stayed and talked for some little time—about the Cotswold country, which he likes immensely—he and Mrs. James stayed at Bibury—and he talked about Bernard Bosanquet,[4] said "He is of the opposite school from myself, but I've always felt more in sympathy with him than with the others of that school." He is a delightful

---

1. Eminent Philadelphia surgeon Dr. J. William White (1850–1916) and his wife.
2. He gave the eight Hibbert Lectures, 4–28 May 1908.
3. Leopold J. Vidler, Rye historian, member of a prominent and influential family in Rye.
4. Bernard Bosanquet (1848–1923), Theodora's cousin, wrote and taught philosophy at University College Oxford, and at St. Andrews University.

man—small and thin—he looks about 10 years older than Mr. Henry
but *is* only 1 year more I believe.

Tuesday, 28 July [1908]. In the afternoon Nora and Miss Peggy James
and I took tea down to Camber and had it among the sand dunes. Miss
PJ is very much interested in psychic phenomena. She says her father
is becoming more and more convinced that there *are* supernatural
agencies—that's very comforting. If only he will work at that side of
psychology one really might hope for results! Miss James hasn't much
sense of humor, which makes her just a bit heavy in hand.

Tuesday, 4 August [1908]. I took my bicycle out for air and exercise
after lunch and rode, via Ledmine, to Hastings and very "up hill and
down dale" sort of ride. At Hastings I went to interview the clairvoy-
ant palmist Mme Troutel. I don't feel sure of her genuineness. She
answered no "test" questions right and made several very bad shots at
other things—but some good ones. However it is all fully typewritten
elsewhere so I won't repeat it here. Had tea afterwards at the oriental
café. Home by train—very weary.

Sunday, 9 August [1908]. I took "The Psychical Phenomenon of Spiritualism"[5] to read at Mr. James', and Professor James saw it, and began
talking about spiritualism. He says a "new era" is dawning in these
matters, and he seems to believe in "Eusapia's" mediumistic powers.[6]
He appears to be intensely interested in the matter.

SIR SIDNEY WATERLOW DIARY
Sunday, 9 August 1908. Lunched with the Protheros. Tea at the Steps.[7]
H. and W. James, the Protheros, Mrs. Ford. Talk about spiritualism.

5. *The Physical Phenomena of Spiritualism* (Boston, 1907) by Hereward Carrington
(1880–1959), American scientist of varied interests and a prolific author.
6. Eusapia Palladino, famous Italian medium who had been attracting international
attention since the turn of the century, in late 1909 and early 1910 was in New
York, where she had come to be at the disposition of Hereward Carrington. William
James visited her with Carrington on 12 January 1910.
7. Alice (Lloyd) Dew-Smith, gardener, author (*The Diary of a Dreamer,* 1900), and
dabbler in psychic phenomena, lived in a cottage just north of Rye—"The Steps"—
which one reached by ascending a long flight of stone steps.

Wednesday, 9 September [1908]. W.J. most kindly lent me the S.P.R.[8] report on Mrs. Holland's automatic writing—which is wonderfully interesting and suggestive. I read part of it aloud to Nellie in the evening and we were both impressed to the point of trying to see if we're the least good ourselves at automatic writing.

Tuesday, 28 October 1913. . . . an interesting passage from a letter of Peggy's about a visit she and her mother paid to a medium in Boston whom Mrs. William and Mrs. Tom Perry[9] are cultivating. The medium, described as an ignorant but honest woman, was in a trance and was, I gather, supposed to be in communication with William James. She said, "I'm carried away to a place where a gentleman is sitting in a chair with wheels. Mr. James says, 'It's my brother.' Now an aunt comes." At this stage Mrs. William James said "Oh which of my dear aunts is it?" To which the medium replied, "No, not your aunt but the aunt of the other, her aunt Alice (the name of Mr. James' sister, dead many years since).[10] She says you are to tell her brother Henry that she saw them give him something and she was very pleased. He was pleased too. A bright bowl. A golden bowl.[11] And she asks him if he ever looks at her face behind a glass."

As Mr. James pointed out to me from his big study chair he has two framed and glazed photographs of his sister in full view. He explained it, as Peggy herself did, purely as telepathy from her subconsciousness to the medium, but I think he had a lurking doubt, a kind of feeling "What if it were really Alice?" all the time.

[Monday], 28 September 1914. No very interesting looking books at the [Free] Library except Hereward Carrington's latest "Problems of Psy-

---

8. The English Society for Psychical Research (SPR) was founded in 1882. William James became a corresponding member in 1884 and organized the American SPR, which merged with the English in 1890—with William James as vice president, a position he held until his death (except for 1894–95, when he was president)—and published occasionally in the society's *Proceedings.*

9. Lilla Cabot (b. 1848) in 1874 married Thomas Sergeant Perry (1845–1928), American critic and editor, and a friend of James's since boyhood.

10. Peggy's aunt, Alice James (1848–1892), sister to William and Henry.

11. The specified gift seems to allude to the birthday present bought by the subscription arranged in England by Edmund Gosse, Percy Lubbock, and Hugh Walpole to honor James's seventieth anniversary, a silver gilt porriger—a golden bowl.

chical Research"[12] which I grabbed at once and read during Mr. James's intervals.

Wednesday, 30 September 1914. It's really a relief to read Hereward Carrington on Psychical Research. He makes one very pointed observation as to the *kind* of person to whom psychical research appeals. It must appeal, that is, mainly to people who have been "inoculated," as it were, with materialism. To anyone who admits readily and *a priori* the existence of a spiritual world, anyone who *feels* certain of it, the methods of psychical research can naturally mean very little and be worth very little. But if one's once been bitten by the scientific dogma that life is a function of the organism and thought a function of the brain, *then* the work of the S.P.R. takes on an immensely greater value. Because apart from the facts of psychical research it has to be admitted that there is no *proof* of the existence of consciousness apart from matter. I'm afraid Nellie will be losing patience if she has even had enough to read as far as this. For the things that penetrate into my own vitals and seem very profoundly and illuminatingly true generally seem to her rather trite truisms. Still, as I want this diary (as far as it goes) to be a sort of general account of one's reactions at the time of writing, this sort of thing has a kind of right to a place in it. Because I must say that reading Carrington's interesting book has revived with a good deal of intensity my own wish to *do* some definite little bit of research, to help along the work to some extent, however slight. I think, in time, I might be a fairly accurate observer of various phenomena. I couldn't ever be any use in the automatic writing work, because one must have a classical education to be able to understand the frequent classical allusions.

I took a No. 19 up to Piccadilly. When I got out I noticed a group of people before the window of the "Occult Library," up a little alley on the North of Piccadilly, so I went to see what they were looking at and found the window devoted to huge (and I think unauthenticated) horoscopes of Kitchener and Churchill,[13] and a long screed which pur-

---

12. *The Problems of Psychic Research* (London and New York, 1914).
13. Horatio Herbert, Lord Kitchener (1850–1916), British military leader. Winston Leonard Spencer Churchill (1874–1965), British statesman, prime minister 1940–45 and 1951–55, was at this time First Lord of the Admirality.

ported to be "Telepathetic War News," the most cautious drivel imaginable. Equally cautious in its way is the copy of "Modern Astrology" which I bought later on at Watkin's. It has a number of interesting horoscopes and was worth getting on their account, but Mr. Alan Leo quite refuses to commit himself to any rash prophecies. He has received a lot of questions about the War, which he prints with his answers at the end of the magazine. "The tone of the answers," he says, "should be studied intuitively." And this is the kind of answer on which intuitions are to be exercised.

Q. "Which will be probable bad periods when reverses etc., are likely? A. Reverses are likely to occur to either side under adverse aspects of Uranus and Saturn to Mars. The progress of Mars should be carefully watched and its effects on the various nations engaged noted. In this way we shall learn more concerning the planets ruling nations."

The "Occult Review," which I got as well, has in full the very curious and apparently quite well authenticated 1854 Prophecy of Mayence, foretelling in considerable detail both the Prussian campaigns of 1866 and 1870 and this present War. I can't quote it here because I've lent the copy to Nora and Rachel for a few days as they were both interested.

Tuesday, 3 August 1915. I came into the long room to do some copying (of W. James' letters to F. W. H. Myers)[14] after tea.

Wednesday, 4 August [1915]. This morning H.J. read me part of a most interesting letter from Mrs. T. S. Perry about a medium she has discovered in her New Hampshire summer village. A very wonderful young woman apparently, even more so, she and her husband think, than Mrs. Piper. But she is a very keen churchwoman and can't bear the fact of her mediumship being known as it would bring her under suspicion among her sect. There were extraordinarily interesting details of a sitting in which John Fiske,[15] the historian, was "imperson-

---

14. Frederick William Henry Myers (1843–1901), one of the founders of the English Society for Psychical Research; he met William James in 1882.
15. John Fiske (1842–1901), American historian and chief popularizer of Victorian philosophy and science in the United States.

ated" in the medium's body, and gave very wonderful proofs of his identity. All this has considerably impressed H.J. and makes him more inclined to pay attention to the message from his brother which was sent over some weeks back, urging him "not to take the step he has in mind." He thought at the time it might refer to going to Rye, but it looks to me much more as if it had connection with his naturalisation as an Englishman.[16] Nellie suggests that we are going to war with America, and that's why. I hope not, but if it were so even, I think H.J. would be so thoroughly on our side in spirit that he couldn't have retained his American citizenship in the event. Anyway, he took that step, so it's too late now.

Tuesday, 16 November 1915. [Mrs. Earp reads Bosanquet's cards:] "New arrangement of life on account of the death of an elderly man." . . .

Horoscope Method: Great changes for better coming into life. Some trouble about papers . . .

Another method: Superficially good luck in 3 months. . . . It looks hopeful for the Letters [her novel] anyway!

Thursday, 11 November 1915. Nellie . . . healed a neuralgic spot on my head with great success before we went out.

Wednesday, 22 December 1915. When I came back [from Carlyle Mansions] I asked Nellie if she thought it would be any good exercising her healing power on Mr. James—whether she could give him an easier night. She said she would try.

Thursday, 23 December 1915. . . . over [to Carlyle Mansions] before breakfast . . . he *had* had a quieter night. . . . This is all to Nellie's credit I firmly believe, for it seems to have been quite a different kind of rest, a much easier mental condition, than he has hitherto shown any signs of. Came back to breakfast.

---

16. Disappointed with American's reluctance to enter the war on the side of the Allies, James had taken the Oath of Allegiance and become a British subject on 26 July 1915; his sponsors were Prime Minister Herbert H. Asquith, Edmund Gosse, J. B. Pinker, and George Prothero.

Theodora Bosanquet at Work, 1920–1960

By the end of the twenties Theodora Bosanquet had gained some recognition in the literary world as a result of her contributions to the *Saturday Westminster Gazette,* her three substantial essays on Henry James in important periodicals, and of course the two editions in England of *Henry James at Work* and a reprint of it in the United States of America. The British government gave her additional recognition with the honor of Member of the British Empire for her work during the Great War and in the immediate postwar years. In 1920 she accepted the position of executive secretary of the International Federation of University Women. The post involved her gratefully in drawing together members of the informal sisterhood of women who had been graduated from colleges and universities around the world, informing them personally of their achievements and making them aware of the as yet unfulfilled professional needs and desires of the international association of the "weaker" or captive sex. It was demanding work, but it afforded the compensation of worldwide travel and expanded experience that such adventure provided. That experience, however, did not draw her completely away from the world of Henry James, thanks to the intrusion of a young man from McGill University. Leon Edel had written to her from Paris in June 1929, and accepted her invitation to visit her in November. Edel has left us this impression of Bosanquet at age forty-nine:

> I found her [in the Chelsea district of London] in a small dim office, a woman of medium height, straight, direct, with clear eyes that I remember as blue; she rose to shake my hand, with a welcoming smile and yet a kind of reticence and distance that were familiar to me, for I had grown up in Canada where we were taught the reverse of American breeziness and instant

camaraderie. She remained behind her desk; I sat opposite her.
. . . She was a model of tact and diplomacy.

Their subsequent correspondence also reflects the compensatory benefit
of travel that her position with the Federation of University Women
afforded. One of her earliest letters to the new Jamesian, dated 16 April
1931, is headed "Wellesley College, Wellesley, Mass." A bit later she
writes to him from "Mina House Hotel, Pyramids, Cairo, December
21, 1933"; after the business news she adds, "This has been a marvelous
tour—Greece—Palestein—Egypt." But further light on the demanding
nature of the job and specifically on its interference with other features
of her personal life and interests is cast by a letter written between the
two just referred to; she has been a dozen years at work as the executive
secretary, and the strain now has begun to show. It is dated 25 September 1932, and begins with an apology to the young Leon Edel—"If I
hadn't been caught and held up all round by an amazing lot of work following the international Conference in Edinburgh, I should have
answered your very interesting letter of August 1st long ago." The second half of the letter contains suggestions about projects involving
Henry James's works—a word to the Macmillan publishing house and
to Percy Lubbock concerning Edel's edition of James's plays; an
omnibus volume of James's shorter stories, with an introduction "based
mainly on the prefaces [to the New York Edition], and partly, for some
of the later, post-preface ones, on my own memories of their respective
origins." Clearly, Bosanquet's interest in Henry James and his work per-
sists, and her desire to be involved in that topic remains quite alive.
Another indication of the way the demands of the Federation intrude on
her more personal interests shows up in the next couple of sentences:

I'm horribly busy with very dull work—or mostly very dull.
The little book I was doing on Paul Valéry got held up—by University Women and their Conferences—and in the meantime,
just when I was committing myself to saying that P.V. wasn't
likely to do any very important new work, he published something that is for him quite a book.[1]

---

1. Valéry's *L'Idée fixe, ou Deux Hommes à la Mer* was privately issued by the Labora-
toires Martinet in 1932.

The little book on Valéry was not Bosanquet's first endeavor of the kind. She had already published a book on Harriet Martineau[2]—the same Harriet who had been attended to and cared for by her ancestral cousins Erasmus "Ras" Darwin and Hensleigh Wedgwood. That was certainly not, of course, the principal point of interest for Bosanquet, although she does rehearse their benevolent efforts on Harriet's behalf. She duly notes that the cousins labored diligently to persuade the government to grant Martineau a Civil List pension, and that their success was crowned with her refusal to accept it. She did, however, deign to accept the subsequent Testimonial Fund that involved several of her friends, and the cousins as joint treasurers. Harriet Martineau was an eccentric, a misfit, at times, an invalid, but she worked heartily on the behalf of feminist interests—equality and social justice. Furthermore, she was a talented and indefatigable writer.

Bosanquet observes early in the book that Harriet was the daughter of a Dissenter descended from "a Huguenot surgeon" (2–3). The surgeon would have struck rather a familiar note in the Bosanquet ear; the Dissenter legacy would have reminded her (as some of her later writings stoutly suggest) of Henry James, Senior, who wanted his children to be able to reject the imposition of educational and other guidelines and related regulations that they had not freely chosen. The strong-minded Martineau was certainly dissenter enough herself and would also have approved of the ideas of Henry's father. Bosanquet notes as well the atypical education of Harriet and her sister Rachel, who attended a boys' school—two generations before Bosanquet attended the atypical Cheltenham Ladies College in the midst of male-only educational institutions in England (19); throughout most of the nineteenth century in England such institutions denied matriculation to women.

Harriet Martineau's atypical schooling contributed to her burgeoning feminist platform. Bosanquet points out that Martineau's attitude insists "women are intelligent beings, and [as a second plank in the platform] she reduces Divinity to utilitarian ethics. . . . Practical Divinity": that is, "admirable conduct, ethics in action." Her brother James Martineau admired and encouraged her: "leave it to other

---

2. *Harriet Martineau: An Essay in Comprehension* (London: Etchells and Hugh Macdonald, 1927). Subsequent references are given in the text.

women to make shirts and darn stockings" while she pursued the path
of female writer. Furthermore, "women could teach morality better
than men" (24–25). Her interest in and finally her commitment to
mesmerism assuredly fascinated Bosanquet, who had more than a nod-
ding acquaintance with the practice. Indeed, she sympathized with
Martineau's commitment to social reform, her embracing all the
causes and all the abused "minorities" (which turned out, as is usually
the case, to be in fact majorities)—women, blacks, "foreigners" (even
on their own colonized native soil), and so forth.

A traveler herself, as executive secretary of the International Federation of University Women, she readily appreciated Martineau's
international experience and sympathies—her functioning as fund-
raiser for Oberlin College in Ohio and the cousinly thrust of her *Society in America* (1839):

> In spite of this disqualification [Martineau's severe deafness], and
> in spite of the difficulties inherent in her plan of measuring
> Americans against the declaration of Independence, the book she
> wrote was a valuable aid to the understanding of a nation peren-
> nially misunderstood by the English. . . . As a picture of Amer-
> ica, [however,] her book was too obviously coloured by the
> creed of the abolitionist. (107)

(I think Bosanquet intended no pun in that reservation.) Bosanquet
also speaks favorably of *The House and the Man,* Martineau's
glorification of the black leader Toussaint-L'Ouverture (135); and she
adds that Martineau's recently acquired (1840) friend Florence
Nightingale found the book "the greatest of historical romance" (136).

In spite of her own deep sympathies with Harriet Martineau's attitudes and ideas, Bosanquet is never distracted by her enthusiasm. Her
commentary is characterized by a level-headed refusal to be totally
carried away by them: there remains in her commentary the steady
leaven of sane skepticism, a sturdy British attitude of *nil admirari,*
quite perceptible in the humor that is always available. Bosanquet was
always interested in spiritualism, paranormal psychological phenomena, and especially perhaps in the mesmerism that so involved Martineau. Yet she shares the hesitation of Martineau's mother to believe
in all the cures effected by mesmeric healing, and she paraphrases that

hesitancy thus: "Drugs and knives were legitimate weapons against disease, but these wavings of hands in the air were contrary alike to divine wisdom and common sense" (154). Harriet, of course, anticipated the pragmatic William James—in effect insisting "the proof of the pudding. . . ."

Bosanquet's gentle skepticism unites with her subtle humor as she relates Martineau's eager response to the handsome mesmerist Henry George Atkinson (whom she met in the town of Lenton, near Nottingham) and their discussions of personal immorality: "After a few more conversations she was ready to emerge from the stifling air of Christian theology into the purer gas provided by the new prophet." She cannot resist adding that Martineau "noticed a remarkable likeness between Mr. Atkinson and Jesus Christ" (157). Finally, a less restrained Bosanquet emerges in her account of Martineau's interest in the U.S. Civil War and the Indian Mutiny and Florence Nightingale's telegram urging her: "'agitate, agitate for Lord and Grey in place of Sir George Lewis.' . . . and she immediately took up her pen and agitated" (208). One is urged, in turn, to say that Bosanquet's *Harriet Martineau: An Essay in Comprehension* succeeded in taking it all in.

The little book *Paul Valéry* (1933) displays to advantage another aspect of Bosanquet's intellectual expertise, specifically her ability to discuss intelligently the dense and spare work of a very demanding and "difficult" French poet (1871–1945). Significantly enough, the book opens with her frank confrontation with the most salient feature of his poetry:

> "You are a very difficult author," said the Director of the French Academy when Paul Valéry took his place in the thirty-eighth Chair as successor to Anatole France. (7)

No stern denial or facile acceptance of the charge by the director, but rather Bosanquet's continuation of the topic, carefully retaining Valéry's stance as he gave the customary eulogy of his predecessor: "he took pains to detach himself from association with an author whose intention could be grasped without trouble. . . . 'Alas, gentlemen, there are [those who] . . . insist that the mind shall work for its pleasures. They propound riddles to us. Inhuman creatures'" (7–8). Having caught the irony in Valéry's utterance, she adopts it and puts it to her own immediate use: "Inhuman creatures . . . who insist that our duty to God and to our neighbor is to try to understand their dark sayings" (8).

There is a discernible echo here of another writer with whom Bosanquet was acquainted and whose modesty matched Valéry's, one who was deemed "difficult," one who confessed, "What I everywhere invoke and absolutely take for granted is the maximum of attention." Clearly Henry James, the Master. She comes to the defense of poet Valéry soon enough, as one upon whom nothing is lost, an idea she had developed earlier in her career: the typical poet is vulnerable to the myriad impressions imposed by the world and obliged to make something of them: ". . . the assault of impressions . . . that . . . set the mind fermenting . . . until the feverish labour of creative expression is achieved. To be a poet is to recognise a host of relations among objects kept easily and unquestioningly apart by the ordinary mind" (8–9). Another discernible echo in these opening pages is of Bosanquet's voice in defense of her own great Man in *Henry James at Work*. We have her defense of his "difficulty" (Inhuman creature!) especially in his works of the Major Phase, and also in her account (in the same place) of James's constant exposure to life's impressions. (And let us keep our ears perked up.)

Bosanquet's book gives thorough coverage to Valéry's publications, especially to his poetry. The final chapter provides a summary review of themes and practices discussed in the preceding six, and it takes into account even his very latest, *"L'Idée fixe, ou Deux Hommes à la Mer"* (published as she was trying to push her book to a close in 1932). That last chapter also laments, persuasively, the contest she discerns in Valéry between the sensitive poet and the censorious intellect. Valéry is

a man who has suffered more than enough in the "affective world." He is a poet, and there is no other way for a poet to live. But the capacity for feeling is accompanied by his deep distrust of feeling. . . .

. . . Resistance to inspiration on the plane of the intellect is much the same thing as resistance to temptation on the plane of morality . . . the method may be responsible for some of his failures to carry beginnings to fruition and for grey patches in his prose. A discipline which is excellent for the youth of a man of

the Mediterranean has its obvious dangers as the man grows to
an age when the resonances of emotion are weakened by a nor-
mal decrease of sensibility. It may be that there is a time to stem
the torrent and a time to clear away the obstacles and encourage
it to flow.

This conclusion is responsibly prepared for by the specific and extensive treatment, the alert examination and legitimately apt illustrations
from Valéry's writings throughout the preceding chapters. There is
clearly a mature, sensitive, and sophisticated mind at work; and
Bosanquet happily has a keen ear for French prosody—including
Valéry's demanding manipulation of the "mute e." A helpful example
of that ability is her observations on a few lines from *La Jeune Parque*—

> Valéry uses all the values of words . . . the orchestral resonance
> of their vowels and the rhythmic dance that can be elaborated
> from the play of consonants. The sharply accented "é's" in the
> first line and the sixth—"élancements de votre éternité," the
> high, harmonic effect of "pur et surnatural" in the third, the
> long-drawn "faire luire au lointain," the reinterated "l's" and
> "m's" . . .[3]

Whatever its value as critical elucidation and appreciation (and I think
it is considerable) of his dense, spare poetry, however, Bosanquet's
commentary—the angle of her approach to Paul Valéry (poet,
philosopher, and psychologist), the active bias of her approval—provides for our present purposes a fruitful avenue of comprehension:
there is a constant if subdued rumor, a subtle but distinct echo of an
earlier voice. In her discussion of Valéry as psychologist are reminders
of another psychological writer, one she knew and in whose defense
she shared:

---

3. Some of the lines in question are these:
   Tous-puissants étrangers, inévitables astres
   Qui daignez faire luire au lointain temporel
   Je ne sais quoi de pur et de surnaturel;
   Vous, qui dans les mortels plongez jusques aux larmes
   Ces souverains éclats, ces invincibles armes,
   Et les élancements de votre éternité. . . . (64–63)

[There are] certain tales in which "Bostonian nymphs" appear to have "rejected English dukes for psychological reasons" . . . [and] I am utterly at a loss to see why . . . a reason, psychological or other is not a subject. . . . A psychological reason is, to my imagination, an object adorably pictorial. . . . There are few things more exciting to me, in short, than a psychological reason.[4]

That is, of course, Bosanquet's own great Man at his fiercely frolicsome best, author of some of the most admired (and admirable) psychological fiction of the opening years of the twentieth century.

That echo identified, it is a simple matter to recognize the figurative pattern indicated by Bosanquet's treatment of, for example, Valéry's *L'Ebauche d'un Serpent,* which introduces "the attack of Being upon Not-Being under the disguise of the gliding form of the serpent in the Garden of Eden" (73). Bosanquet's explication of this necessary attack—"necessary" to awaken the Eve figure to the reality of worldly existence—very closely rehearses a constant pattern in the fiction of Henry James. That pattern is the dominant motif of John Milton's *Paradise Lost* and *Paradise Regained,* of William Blake's *Songs of Innocence and Experience* and *The Book of Thel,* of Nathaniel Hawthorne's *The Marble Faun,* and of James's great novels of his Major Phase—*The Wings of the Dove, The Ambassadors, The Golden Bowl,* and the revised version of *The Portrait of a Lady* (1908). The motif is that of the *felix culpa,* the Fortunate (or Fruitful) Fall, an expression of the necessary Fall from the condition of virginal Innocence (the condition of Eve up to the appearance of the seductive serpent) into the world of Experience where Evil exists and where one has the opportunity (having eaten of the fruit of the Tree of the Knowledge of Good and Evil) to see, recognize, and experience the new element, Evil, and to distinguish it from and embrace Good. That leads one, as it does Isabel Archer (in the revised *Portrait of a Lady*), to a new and superior Innocence, into maturity or "salvation"—salvation for life in this world.[5]

---

4. "The Art of Fiction" (1884), fourth-last paragraph of the essay. Such a coincidence of interest must have included Leon Edel (with Bosanquet) during these years when he was just discovering the "psychological reason" as keystone to his biography of James.
5. A reminder of how that motif functions in the last of James's "Major" novels is offered in Lyall H. Powers's *The Portrait of a Lady: Maiden, Woman, and Heroine* (Boston: Twayne, 1991), especially in chapter 6.

Of course, Bosanquet rightly sees that *L'Ebauche d'un Serpent* expresses the act of poetic creation. The serpent is attracted to the lovely, unawakened virgin Eve and begins her seduction; "at the moment when Eve abandons resistance and stretches out her hand, the poet, shedding the serpent's skin, breaks into praise of the Tree of Knowledge" (76). *La Pythie* employs a related motif—"another account of creative energy breaking its way through that pure virginity [resembles] . . . the special creation of poetry, a divine spirit wandering in the flesh of words" (80)—a complement to *L'Ebauche* as James's stories of artists complement his stories on the International Theme.

On receipt of a copy of her book, Valéry wrote to Bosanquet from Florence on 20 May 1933:

Ce livre me paraît exact et excellent. Tout le V. [Valéry] connaissable s'y trouve, habilement et consciencieusement résumé. Les proportions des parties consacrées aux oeuvres diverses, la composition de la suite des analyses que vous en faites, sont très remarquables, et parmi les nombreux miroirs que la critique a bien voulu ajouter à tous les lookings-glasses [*sic*] que je me suis faits, celui-ci est l'un des plus nets et des plus limpides.

Much of the remainder of the letter is a mild chastising of critics (including Bosanquet) who try to "discover" poets within their works—a private and hidden matter, he suggests. A graceful conclusion follows. She might have fared worse![6]

---

6. This letter is in the Bosanquet archive of the Houghton Library, Harvard University. My translation of the letter:

The book seems to me accurate and excellent. All of the V. [Valéry] one might know is there, skillfully and conscientiously gathered together. The relationship among the sections devoted to the various works, the organization of the series of analyses you have made of them, are quite remarkable, and among the numerous mirrors that criticism has deigned to add to all the looking glasses I myself have made, this is one of the purest and clearest.

And of the graceful conclusion, "Voilà, Mademoiselle, quelques remarques que je me permets de vous addresser à titre de remerciement avec mes hommages et mes respectueux souvenirs. Paul Valéry / en voyage—" ("There you are, Mademoiselle, a few remarks that I take the liberty of sending you by way of thanks, along with my gratitude and respectful remembrance. Paul Valéry / abroad—").

Bosanquet's understanding of and sympathy with Valéry's poetry do seem to have benefited from her freshly awakened memory of Henry James and his achievement. That awakening may be attributed, in part at least, to the intrusion of the young Jamesian from McGill, Leon Edel, now at the Sorbonne preparing his thesis on James's "Dramatic Years."

Among the various phenomena that intervened in her life between the publication of *Harriet Martineau* and the publication of *Paul Valéry*, two seem to stand out, to be related, and to demand a special word of commendation. One was the appearance on her doorstep of the young Leon Edel in November 1929; the other was her decision to find a new venue for her creative energies. She was no longer in the blush of youth, was indeed now into her fifties and eager to quit the travel and busyness demanded by the job of executive secretary of the Federation of University Women. Her goal now was to settle down with freedom to do her own creative work. An opportunity to reach that goal came with an invitation to join—if only temporarily, to begin with—the staff of the already prestigious weekly *Time and Tide* as literary editor. She informed Edel, in her letter to him of 21 November 1935,

> I have changed my way of life . . . having migrated from SW3 to NW3 [London postal codes] in close proximity to Hampstead Heath. I've left off being Secretary to the University Women's Federation too. Fifteen years of it was, I thought enough. I'm hoping to do a little study and writing in what leisure years human mortality and the European situation may permit. . . . I'm busy being literary adviser (and pro tem acting as literary editor) to the weekly review *Time and Tide*.

That review (often referred to as simply the "paper") was the brainchild of Margaret Haig Thomas, Lady Rhondda (1883–1958), only daughter of David Alfred Thomas, Viscount Rhondda (1856–1918). He was a successful director of South Wales Coalfield, an industrious and effective public servant, and a cabinet minister during World War I (president of what became the Ministry of Health). Daughter Margaret, second Viscountess Rhondda of Llanwern, became her father's right-hand man and private secretary. In the last year of the Great War she accepted a post in the Ministry of National Service, which included enlistment in the WAACs (Womens Army Auxiliary Corps).[7] After the Armistice she confided in Mrs. Chalmers Watson, founder and first commandant of the WAACs, that her fondest dream was to found a weekly paper, and later added that *"Time and Tide* to-day has many of the features of that paper. . . . Year by year it grows more like the sketch I made then."[8] That comfortable recognition was exactly contemporary with Bosanquet's publication of her book on Valéry and her being on the verge of joining the review following the premature death of Winifred Holtby, its editor.

Holtby shared the principles of Lady Rhondda as pacifist, feminist, liberal internationalist, and journalist. The two women met in 1924; Holtby joined the paper in 1926, to become "the youngest and most active director of *Time and Tide.*"[9] She expressed her pacifist attitude in pithy brevity: "Those who prepare for war get it. There's never been a lack of men willing to die bravely. The trouble is to find a few to live sensibly" (quoted in Brittain, *Testament of Friendship,* 124–25). Holtby bore testimony to the stout yeomanry of her north-country ancestry—the common sense, staunch independence of mind, and straightforward approach that provided a basis for her human sympathy. As those qualities were the foundation of her pacifism, so were they of her feminism—a term she responded to only to reject it:

> I am a feminist because I dislike everything that feminism implies. I desire an end to the whole business, the demands for equality, the suggestion of sex warfare, the very name of feminist. . . . But while inequality exists, while injustice is done and opportunity is denied to the great majority of women, I shall have to be a feminist with the motto Equality First. And I shan't be happy till I get . . . a society in which sex-differentiation concerns those things alone which by the physical laws of nature it must govern, a society in which men and women work together for the good of all mankind, a society in which there is no respect

---

7. See Margaret Haig Thomas, Lady Rhondda, *This Was My World* (London: Macmillan, 1933), 268.

8. Rhondda, *My World,* 301–2.

9. Quoted in Vera Brittain, *Testament of Friendship: The Story of Winifred Holtby* (New York: Macmillan, 1940), 124–25.

of persons, male or female, but a supreme regard for the importance of the human being.[10]

Winifred Holtby was in agreement with Lady Rhondda and her staff on all essential points. Viscount Rhondda had believed that "Democratic government is at best the lesser of two evils . . . it is easily swayed and led by the fluent speaker rather than by the men of caution and capacity. Froth rises to the top, and the person who carries his brain in his tongue is the chosen leader."[11] The report of his daughter, Viscountess Rhondda, implies the shared appreciation of education; for beneath the surface condemnation of the gullibility of the populace there is the profound desire for the welfare of humankind. That general attitude was shared not only among people like Lady Rhondda, her father, and Winifred Holtby, but also by the Darwin-Wedgwood ancestors of Theodora Bosanquet—and by Bosanquet herself.

Winifred Holtby's biographer Vera Brittain wrote on the twentieth anniversary of the paper, just five years after Holtby's death, that "the odds . . . were heavily against success, since the same people for whom the paper was provided—the people who talked the same language as herself [Lady Rhondda]—were only a small group at best."[12] The suggestion seems to be, however, that the number who spoke that language was greater than anticipated, for *Time and Tide* endured and flourished for a couple of decades.

During Theodora Bosanquet's tenure at *Time and Tide,* as literary editor until 1943 and then as a director, the names of contributors to the weekly constitute a rather impressive list and attest to its quality and nature: John Betjeman, C. Day Lewis, T. S. Eliot, Aldous Huxley, C. E. M. Joad, Arthur Koestler, Rose Macaulay, Desmond MacCarthy, Malcolm Muggeridge, George Orwell, Naomi Royde Smith, William Saroyan, Stephen Spender, Enid Starkie, Evelyn Underhill, Rebecca West (a founder), and C. V. Wedgwood (a distant cousin). The range of Bosanquet's contributions to *Time and Tide* covered spiritualist and occult matters, psychology, psychic and other paranormal

10. From an article for the *Yorkshire Post,* quoted in Brittain's *Testament of Friendship,* 127.
11. Rhondda, *My World,* 181.
12. Brittain, *Testament of Friendship,* 133–34.

experience, and of course literature—with especial emphasis on Henry James. And during the *Time and Tide* years she continued her encouragement and nurturing of the young Jamesian Edel.

The persistence of her interest in the occult and paranormal is reflected in the number and quality of her articles on that topic. Williams James's visit to his brother at Lamb House during the summer of 1908 gave her the cherished opportunity to converse with him on the topic of his expertise and so to confirm her in her own interests therein. Now, a generation later, a substantial two-part review article on Laurence J. Bendit's *Paranormal Cognition* demonstrates her progress in that interest.[13] It makes an authoritative, responsible, and sane case for broader academic notice in and official recognition of the topic indicated in Bendit's title. The book was developed from his thesis for the degree of Doctor of Medicine from Cambridge University. Bosanquet traces briefly the developing respectability of such scientific pursuits over the preceding twenty years, mentioning the work of scholars like Whateley Carington, G. N. M. Tyrrel, S. G. Soal, and others. She also cites two significant journals, the American *Journal of Parapsychology* and *The Proceedings of the Society for Psychic Research;* Bosanquet was closely associated (as was William James) with the SPR and, for the decade of the 1930s, was editor of their journal. In the second part of her review she says, "Dr. Bendit's thesis on Paranormal Cognition adds something like a horizontal dimension to the deep vertical shaft into the unconscious sunk by Dr. Jung and his followers." Bosanquet is modestly hopeful.

It was not until Dr. Jung and his followers set about sinking those vertical shafts through the mind of Western man that the value of that heritage [the "spiritual and psychological heritage of the Christian era"] was rediscovered for psychology. When a psycho-therapist of Dr. Jung's experience can say that among all his patients over thirty-five years old "there has not been one whose problem in the last resort was not that of finding a religious outlook on life . . . and none of them has been really healed who did not recover his religious outlook," he is making an impressive statement. Can we afford to disregard it? (415)

---

13. *Time and Tide,* 6 May 1944, 393; and 13 May 1944, 415.

An appropriate complement to that review essay is Bosanquet's review of G. N. M. Tyrrel's *The Personality of Man* in which she praises—and requires—the careful methods of responsible research—"observing facts, examining witnesses, analyzing evidence and devising fraud-proof experiments" (20 September 1947, 1002). She notes that a Chair of Marxism has just been established at Leipzig and an Institute for Dialectical Materialism at Jena; she concludes with a modestly vigorous rhetorical flourish—"Why not a chair of Psychical Research at Cambridge and an Institute of Parapsychology at Oxford?" (1002).

Of course she found occasion to devote a substantial review to a selection of William James's *Writings on Psychology,* ed. Margaret Knight, in *Time and Tide* for Saturday (it always came out on Saturday) 3 March 1951 (XXXIII no. 9, pp. 190–91). Theodora refers to the older brother of her "own great Man" as the "true parent of the restless adolescent science we call modern psychology"; but now her interesting focus on parentage in the review is on Henry James, Sr.—a focus we have come to recognize as her constant concern in writing about the Jameses. William had "an almost perfect father," she affirms, "a liberal-minded enthusiast who invariably encouraged his five children to see things for themselves, think for themselves, and express their ideas in as free a fashion as ever they liked, without ever telling them that 'father knew best.' Although his own life had been profoundly influenced by the writings of Swedenborg, he refrained from proselytizing in the family circle" (190)—as befitted a true Swedenborgian, she might have added.[14]

One of Theodora Bosanquet's deepest commitments was to literature. Her earliest piece is a review of Caroline Spurgeon's landmark *Shakespeare's Imagery and What It Tells Us* (2 November 1935, 1582, 1584), an intelligent and informed evaluation with useful examples of what was truly a singularly significant moment in Shakespeare criticism. Bosanquet would later review, sensitively and sensibly, *The Collected Stories of Katherine Mansfield* (23 February 1946, 181): reading these stories, she claims, "we see the picture, we hear the extraordi-

---

14. A helpful coda to this brief look at Bosanquet's interests is provided by Pamela Thurschwell in her "Henry James and Theodora Bosanquet: On the Typewriter, *In the Cage,* at the Ouija Board," *Textual Practice* 1, no. 1 (1999): 5–23.

narily illuminating talk. These are real people behaving as they are dri-
ven by their instinct and temperament." She quotes Mansfield to Virginia Woolf: "we have the same job, Virginia, and it is really very curious and thrilling that we should both, quite apart from each other, be
after so very nearly the same thing." Bosanquet recognizes that at that
moment (1917) Mansfield and Woolf "shared a vision of life shining
through a rich variety of translucent veils and both were eager to
extend their knowledge and communicate their vision."

Bosanquet's authority as commentator on Woolf is further
strengthened by a little series of pieces on Leslie Stephen's literary
daughter. The most important, from the point of view of *Time and
Tide,* was surely her substantial review of the staunch feminist declaration *Three Guineas* (4 June 1938, 788, 790). Bosanquet there calls it
"the book of the year . . . a revolutionary bomb of a book, delicately
aimed at the heart of our mad armament bidden world . . . a letter to
a professional man, a barrister, on the part women, in particular
'daughters of educated men,' cannot play in the prevention of war"
(788). The quotation there from Lady Rhondda's Hogarth Essay
Leisured Women, published a decade earlier (and repeated frequently
throughout the review) resonates with all of the viscountess's vigor
and feminist condemnation of wasted lives. Bosanquet joins her voice
to Woolf's admonition to these daughters:

> Make it clear that fame and honours and riches have no value in
> your eyes. Refuse homage to nationalist idlers, to old school ties
> and every other "unreal loyalty." . . .
> . . . Why should they applaud the absurd figures Mrs. Woolf
> sees scrambling in the public circus? Educated men, struggling
> for stars and stripes [*sic*] for robes and garters, for white wigs and
> jewelled chains of office, advertising their importance by their
> clothes and their quaint ceremonies. [*Three Guineas* is effectively
> provided with photographs to illustrate Woolf's point.] Little
> boys, dressing up to look distinguished and important.

Bosanquet's passion carries her on to the invocation of a religious
question: Woolf "doesn't believe that 'God made women to match
men.' She has never thought so badly of women as that" (790).

David Daiches's little book *Virginia Woolf* receives just praise in

Bosanquet's review of 21 July 1945 (607), although she attacks the racist-sexist view she claims Daiches got from Coleridge—that artists are androgynous—and his application of that *aperçu* to Woolf's fictional novelist Mary Carmichael. She dispatches Daiches's mild appraisal of Woolf's artistry—"Her techniques are not easily isolated or imitated"—and recommends instead the example of Winifred Holtby (Bosanquet's immediate predecessor at *Time and Time*), "who gave us an excellent description of the methods she employed to write of time and personality—the cinematographic pattern of *Jacob's Room,* the orchestration of *Mrs. Dalloway.*"[15]

At the beginning of that year Bosanquet contributed a personal essay in another genre, although actually a review of memoirs, *Remembering My Good Friends* by Mary Agnes Hamilton (née Adamson). It is a gentle and sympathetic review (13 January 1945, 36), and immediately interesting for the way Bosanquet chooses to evaluate her subject's character: "A lifelong worshipper of Henry James, she has faithfully followed his maxim: 'Try to be one of those on whom nothing is lost.'" The touchstone here is impressive—and most significant.

Bosanquet had been reinvolved in Henry James since the beginning of her participation in Dr. Leon Edel's pursuit of the Master, his letter in the summer of 1929 and then, accepting her invitation, in November. As that pursuit became fruitful and more demanding, her involvement grew deeper and more engrossing. She began supplying him with important papers, suggestions for fruitful personal resources, her own memories, and generous selections from her personal diary from her years at Lamb House and at 21 Carlyle Mansions. Her letter of recommendation, along with one from Edith Wharton, to the Guggenheim Foundation enabled Edel to win a prestigious fellowship and then a continuation of it to work on his edition of James's plays. By no means the only source of her recall of her years from 1907 to 1920, Edel's persistence was certainly a way to keep memories of Rye and Chelsea warm and vital.

---

15. Winifred Holtby, *Virginia Woolf* (London: Wishart, 1932); see chap. 6, "Cinematograph" (on *Jacob's Room*), 116–36, and chapter 7, "The Adventure Justified" (on *Mrs. Dalloway* and *To the Lighthouse* as well), 137–60.

Her first piece on James for *Time and Tide,* 17 April 1943, was called "The Country of Henry James" (316–17), and its immediate justification was to mark the centennial anniversary of his birth. The subtitle and opening sentences seem calculated to set the proper focus and necessary emphasis, to leave nothing to chance. The piece might well have been entitled "The Orientation of Henry James." It recognizes with blessed acuity the role played in that orientation by Henry James, Sr.'s interest in Emmanuel Swedenborg and in François Marie Charles Fourier. It offers, further, a refurbished defense and persuasive explanation of Henry Jr.'s naturalization as a British subject; and, finally, it effectively dismisses the early and misguided *The Pilgrimage of Henry James* (1925) offered by Van Wyck Brooks. The little essay is, in fact, a useful complement to *Henry James at Work* itself, and as such deserves republication here.

THE COUNTRY OF HENRY JAMES
(Born April 15, 1843—Died February 28, 1916)

He was born in New York, an American. He died in London, a British citizen, Henry James, O.M.

The news that sped across the Atlantic in July, 1915, that he had changed his nationality and taken the oath of allegiance to King George V, caused more commotion in his native country than he had expected. American citizens were shocked, even outraged. They took it as a criticism—the most extreme criticism conceivable—of the United States' neutrality. Henry James, regretfully aware of the uproar, permitted himself to remark that America had a "great doctrine that to invite scores and scores of millions of aliens to naturalize themselves with *her* is in the highest degree exemplary and edifying" and yet "any such proceeding on the part of her own children elsewhere deserves but signal reprobation."

It was a proceeding that would hardly have occurred to him if America had been a fighting Ally in 1915, but it was not so much a criticism of the United States as a simple desire to be completely at one with the country where he had lived for forty years. The discovery that he could only visit his own house in Rye on the footing of an Alien, under police supervision, was the occasion of his decision to apply for nationality, but no more than an occasion. He wanted, as he explained to his nephew, "to rectify a position that has become inconveniently and uncomfortably false."

The reprobation that greeted his action has hardly ceased even yet, and its scope has been enlarged to include the forty years' domicile as well. At least one book has been written to support the perverse thesis that Henry James made the mistake of his life when he expatriated himself. His answer would have been that he never did expatriate himself. He was reasonably sure that he had found his country here without losing America. As he wrote his brother in 1888 (see p. 56, note 51):

> I can't look at the English-American world, or feel about them, any more, save as a big Anglo-Saxon total, destined to such an amount of melting together that an insistence on their differences becomes more and more idle and pedantic; and that melting together will come faster the more one takes it for granted and treats the life of the two countries as continuous or more or less controvertible, or at any rate as simply different chapters of the same general subject. . . . I have not the least hesitancy in saying that I aspire to write in such a way that it would be impossible to an outsider to say whether I am at a given moment an American writing about England or an Englishman writing about America (dealing as I do with both countries), and so far from being ashamed of such an ambiguity I should be exceedingly proud of it, for it would be highly civilized.

If he never quite hit that target, it was because he surpassed it, because he never could have written his criticism of life as a mere American or a mere Englishman, but only and increasingly as his unique self, Henry James. Highly civilized he was, apparently from childhood. His father had seen to that. Henry James the elder was a passionately religious philosopher who devoted book after book to his own original and unconventional interpretation of a doctrine inspired by Swedenborg. The other star in his firmament was Fourier, whose schemes for the reconstruction of human society on a cooperative basis filled in the empty spaces in the cosmic drama of man's relation with God. It was in 1847, when his second son was four years old, that the elder Henry James came in contact with enthusiastic Fourierists in New York. He became a frequent contributor to their periodicals and was known among them as "Henry James the Seer." He wore the mantle of prophet modestly but quite easily. What he foresaw was the speedy regeneration of mankind, not by any revolution of malcontents but by a universal change of heart. The brotherhood of man was for him a simple reality, temporarily obscured by greed and competition. He had the lowest opinion of a society in which philanthropy was the prerogative of the rich and privileged. As he wrote to a friend: "I have been so long accustomed to see the most arrant deviltry transact itself in the name of benevolence that the moment I hear a profession of good-will from almost any quarter I instinctively look about for a constable or place my hand within reach of the bell-rope. . . . no man can play the Deity to his fellow man with hope of impunity—I mean spiritual impunity of course. . . . I do hope the reign of benevolence is over: until that event occurs I am sure the reign of God will be impossible."

The higher and cloudier flights of paternal speculation seem to have floated over the head of the young Henry James, but he caught onto the tail of the Fourier kite. His friend, T. S. Perry, writing about the conversational walks he and the fifteen year old Henry enjoyed in 1858, remembered a Lily Pond as the scene of a long discussion about "Fourier's plan for regenerating the world. Harry had heard his father describe the great reformer's proposal to establish universal happiness, and like a good son he tried to carry the good news farther." Henry James's father was, in fact, the only continuous educational influence he was exposed to throughout his youth, for the minds of the young Jameses were trained on a curious plan. Knowledge had to be injected, but they were not stamped with the imprint of any school or master. The procession of tutors in England, France and Switzerland, the short spells of work in schools from which the boys were lifted before they had time to sink the tiniest rootlets in the soil, would have scandalized English parents of the period. The American parent seemed to favor chopping and changing without limit. He took pains never to cramp his children's freedom or impose his "ideas" on them, but he lived with them, he traveled with them, he was always there, a genial, powerful presence, and his sons loved him.

This persistent presence had its effect. To his father's influence and example Henry James owed some at least of the penetrating ethical insight characteristic of all his work. As Newton Arvin put it, in an admirable essay on *Henry James and the Almighty Dollar,* he saw with deadly lucidity "the corrupt life of the great bourgeoisie, or the philistine morals of the small bourgeoisie of his time." If his observations of the sin of greed were made in a European setting, it was not because he was unaware that it was actively at work in America. The emancipation of the human heart from sin so confidently anticipated by his father, was still, it seemed, some way off. Most people were neither kind nor generous nor just and what passed for tolerance was no better than cynical indifference. Covetousness, treachery and tyranny were in the ascendant, though they still, in that day, found it convenient to wear hypocritical masks cast in the mould of virtue. Henry James devoted careful attention to the delicate operation of tracing the hideous features sheltering behind those masks. His novels and tales are more often than not exposures of ferociously greedy persons engaged in fleecing or exploiting a small minority of innocent, friendly and imaginative persons—the tiny, scattered band of the truly civilized. That was the theme of his early work as it was of his latest unfinished novel, *The Ivory Tower.*

But why, if the sins of an acquisitive society were his prime subject, did he feel compelled to leave America? The answer may well be that under his father's guidance he had spent much of his most impressionable years acquiring a taste for Europe. The style and architecture of Europe could feed his immense visual appetite as the sights of America couldn't. Civilization was kindness and courtesy, but it was also permanence and tradition. In Europe, in England particularly, the traditional pattern might be so rubbed and faint that it took an uncommonly perceptive eye to appreciate it, but that was precisely the kind of eye that Henry James had. Life in England and America might be "merely different chapters of the same general subject," but under the English chapter was richer in its backward reach.

Yet he did not intend, when he came over in 1875, to settle in England. His Europe was made up of five countries: Switzerland, Italy, Germany, France, and England. Switzerland was a holiday resort for children and mountaineers. Italy was a lovely romance, an enchantment for repeated visits, but not (the Browning legend notwithstanding) a country for a writer to live and work in. Germany he had already ruled out. In 1872 he wrote: "I can never hope to become an unworthiest adoptive child of the fatherland. It is well to listen to the voice of the spirit, to cease hair-splitting and treat oneself to a good square antipathy—when it is so very sympathetic!" His brother William, who knew Germany far more intimately, was mis-led into believing that "the people are a good safe fact for great pow-ers to be entrusted to." He could write in 1910 of "the strong, calm, successful new German civilization." But Henry James had summed up Germany in one of the characters sketched in *A Bundle of Letters* (1879). In this ironic little study of tourists in a Paris pension, Dr. Rudolf Staub, the German Professor who is using his "good, square German head" to analyse his table companions, French, English and American, and to misinterpret them with Teutonic assurance, writes to a colleague at Göttingen:

It is interesting in this manner to perceive, so largely developed, the germ of extinction in the so-called powerful Anglo-Saxon family. . . . Add to this that there are two young Englanders in the house, who hate the Americans in a lump, making between them none of the distinctions and favourable comparisons which they insist upon, and you will, I think, hold me warranted in believing that, between precipitate decay and internecine enmi-ties, the English-speaking family is destined to consume itself, and that with its decline the prospect of general pervasiveness will brighten for the deep-lunged children of the Fatherland.

The country that had seemed to beckon to Henry James in advance as his predestined home was France. There was French civilization, there was Paris. Paris was the place in the world where writers could live at ease, the city where art and letters were treated as a serious, hon-ourable, necessary part of life. He took rooms in Paris once; but as time went on he discovered it was impossible to stay there perma-nently. He was a stranger, he would always be a stranger. French writers, exemplary though they were, struck him as far too well satisfied with their own closed circle. He came to know several of them well, he admired them, but he couldn't unite with them. "Chi-nese, Chinese, Chinese!" he exclaimed, a few years later. Paris was their Celestial Empire and all the world beyond was, for them, outer darkness inhabited by barbarians.

So he came to England and the longer he stayed the more sure he was that he had taken the right step. The English might be (they often were) exasperating, they had minds like glue-pots, they were philistine, but they were his own people. When he suggested to Edith Wharton that she would do well to leave France and live in England, he assured her that it was the real field of extension for an American, that a Franco-American life must be, however alluring, comparatively sterile. (Mrs. Wharton didn't take his advice, she said there was no conversation in England.) For Henry James the sense of kinship grew closer with each passing year. He suffered, at recurrent intervals, when England's "prestige" appeared once more to be lost; he sometimes found himself wishing the cautious, compromising country would show fight, even in a bad cause, "if only to show that she still can, and that she is not one vast, money-getting Birmingham." He had terrible moments in the summer of 1914 while he "sought certitude" that his faith in the British genius was justified. But as war broke and thundered, he was lifted on a great wave of sympathy and confidence. The British people had not failed. They were brave, they were loyal, they were dogged. Their skulls might be thick and their tongues slow, but they were all right, they had character. They were generous; they were hospitable. Look at the way they welcomed hosts of refugees! He left the unendurable country sunshine for London so that he could help to look after the refugees. He placed his pen and his name at the service of volunteer ambulances. He worked on committees. To go through the formality of naturalization as a British citizen was just to add the seal to a signature written through the years and abundantly honoured.

THE GARDEN-ROOM
EXTRACT FROM *Henry James: The War Chapter*
By Leon Edel

At right angles to Lamb House stood the garden-room where Henry James dictated most of his later novels and essays. It was a house apart, in substantial and tawny-coloured brick, but consisting only of one long room. The novelist, as he paced the floor

and measured out his sonorous sentences to the accompanying
tick of Theodora Bosanquet's typewriter, could see from large
windows at one end the irregular old street; from the others he
looked out at the carefully kept garden. Lamb House proper was
his home . . . The garden-room was the inner sanctum: his visitors, sitting in the garden, could hear in the morning his old
voice rising, falling, and pausing in the fashioning of his complicated sentences. It was the novelist's laboratory, where at fixed
hours of the day, uninterrupted, and adhering rigidly to his rou-
tine, he could perform his alchemy of words.

This sanctuary and ivory tower of the Master was in the old
Sussex town of Rye . . . In its sky, in the last days of August,
1940, there appeared the raiders, they swept high over the red
roof-tops, flying in a straight line, and dropped their sticks of
bombs through the clear air of the old town. One bomb scored
a direct hit on Henry James's garden-room. . . .

Bosanquet contributed another half dozen articles on James to *Time
and Tide*—on James and his works and friends; the articles show that
she kept abreast of scholarly and critical books about the Jamesian
world. First, and of considerable importance, is her review of F. O.
Matthiessen's *Henry James: The Major Phase* (21 December 1946, 1244,
1246). She welcomes the appearance of serious James criticism and
the light it throws on "the changing outlook of thoughtful citizens of
the United States." That change, she surmises, "began as a healthy
reaction to a lively irritant, Mr. Van Wyck Brooks's Pilgrimage of
Henry James." Furthermore, she acknowledges the "astonishing piece
of good fortune" Matthiessen enjoyed by being able to read James's
personal notebooks covering the years 1878 to 1914. Oddly enough,
she seems to have been unaware that Leon Edel had enjoyed the same
good fortune—thanks to the impression made by his *Les Années drama-
tiques* on Harry James (William's son)—at a date a decade earlier.
Edel found the notebooks in an old sea-chest in Harvard's Widener
Library in the summer of 1937 (with the family's permission to rum-
mage there), and was obviously struck by the entry for Valentine's
Day 1895. That entry confirmed the basic assumption of his M.A. thesis at McGill and of his *Thèse principale* at the Sorbonne; there James is
pondering the trauma of his failure as a dramatist in the 1890s and
realizes he has learned a grateful lesson: "the precious lesson . . . *of the*

singular value for a narrative plan too of the . . . divine principal of the
Scenario . . . a key that, working in the same *general* way fits the complicated chambers of *both* the dramatic and the narrative lock."[16] It was
a hectic time for Edel, and a variety of other demands may well have
distracted him from informing Bosanquet of his luck at Harvard. In
any case, such information is missing from their correspondence.

Matthiessen's attention to the late novels, and particularly his
regarding *The Portrait of a Lady* as James's masterpiece (quite literally)
and correctly approving of its revision for publication in 1908—to
take its proper place—gets Bosanquet's praise. But his rating *The
Golden Bowl* as markedly inferior to *The Wings of the Dove* and *The
Ambassadors* raises her hackles. She gapes at Matthiessen's attitude: "he
finds it magnificent but hollow." Then Bosanquet persuasively
accounts for Maggie Verver as a heroine who "has to embody virtue
triumphant without herself either dying or in any other way escaping
from the stage. . . . Her force is love, an all-embracing love which Mr.
Matthiessen finds distasteful. There is, he suggests, 'something slightly
sickening in this wide-open declaration of being in love with love,
without discrimination between kinds.'" The next paragraph is as
stern—and as brilliant—as Bosanquet needs to be:

Here we seem to touch a difference between Henry James's values and Mr. Matthiessen's, a difference which makes him judge
that James could strike only the "minor chords," those of "renunciation, or resignation, of inner triumph in the face of defeat." It
is a fundamental difference, leading us to wonder whether the
majority of artists wouldn't disagree with Mr. Matthiessen.
(1244)

Matthiessen is allowed to work his way into her good graces with his
chapter on Henry James's philosophy and religion—or lack of it. "It is
particularly valuable for placing Henry James in vital relationship with
his gifted and abundantly inspired father as well as with the problem of
good and evil" (1244).

---

16. The italics are James's. While some post-Edel biographers misquote the "lesson" as "the principle of the divine Scenario," the quotation—"divine principle"—is
as James wrote it. See *Complete Notebooks,* 115.

Bosanquet provides a sound appreciation of James's "first" novel, *Roderick Hudson,* in her review of its reprinting, "Roderick and Roland," in *Time and Tide* (21 June 1947, 661–62). There she boldly (and rightly) disagrees with Michael Swan's notion that James valued this one above *The Portrait of a Lady.* But she gives *Roderick* its due, finally, as "a lively, dramatic story"; and in the last sentence of her review also gives the back of her gloved hand to her favorite misguided critic, carefully camouflaged, of course: "It is also, for anyone properly interested in the pilgrimage of Henry James [*sic*], an indispensable introduction to his work" (662). A similarly sound reading of a new printing of *What Maisie Knew* (29 November 1947, 1276–78), gives Bosanquet the opportunity to chastise once again the thesis of Van Wyck Brooks—reinforced by the approval of V. L. Parrington—in her crisp and fulsome prose.

The Scenery [in *Maisie*] may indeed be European, but where do most of those gallant, innocent, betrayed yet triumphant heroes and heroines come from? . . . Americans, with all their crudities, had the supreme virtue of youth; they were open, more than Europeans, to the assaults of experience. The greedy, corrupt world could be represented through their eyes even better than through the eyes of a child, such a child as Maisie, for instance. (1277)

A triumphant note, however, dominates her review of the initial volume of Edel's biography, *Henry James: The Untried Years, 1843–1870* (21 December 1953, 888). The note is very like that of a gratified surrogate mother. The parental metaphor is not absolutely *outré:* Bosanquet entitled her review "The Son and the Brother." She makes an interesting comparison between Edel's biographical volume and James's autobiographical volumes (*A Small Boy and Others,* and *Notes of a Son and Brother):* the two items cover the same twenty-seven years as Edel's *Untried Years.*[17] Bosanquet very quickly moves, in the review, to Henry Sr.: "The eccentric factor in this family was the

---

17. Bosanquet would review F. W. Dupee's *The Autobiography of Henry James* (the first two completed volumes and the unfinished third, *The Middle Years*) just three years later. She there repeats the similarity between the autobiographical volumes and Edel's biography and also the inspirational value of "Father's ideas."

father"; she makes intelligent reference (as she had previously) to the importance of Swedenborg and Fourier in his life and in that of the family. "For the rest of his life [from 1844 on] he thought and wrote and talked his own version of Swedenborg wedded with his own version of Fourier prophesying the advent of a society of uncorrupted men and women inspired by the love of God and their fellows." Her final touch to complete the portrait of the father, is this—"Thanks to being his father's son, Henry James was able to start on his line uncommonly early."

One more major item is the two-part article of 1954, "As I Remember—Henry James" (3 July, 875–76; 10 July, 913–14). This is basically a reprise of the material of *Henry James at Work* (thirty years later) with a few additional details and some amplification.

Soon after the end of World War II Bosanquet had become a personage of some importance, and her career with *Time and Tide* found a parallel in her role of public speaker. She was involved with the BBC and the halls of academe—again principally as an authority on the life and work of Henry James. A note struck in both her BBC talk in early 1947, for their series Studies in English Letters and called simply "Henry James," and again in the Founder's Memorial Lecture at Girton College (October 1947) entitled "The Return of Henry James," would be echoed in much later appreciations of James's fiction. The BBC piece treats James's "determination to proclaim the necessity of art and the supreme importance of aesthetic awareness":

> He does it more often than not by placing someone who is at least a potential artist somewhere in the story. . . . Sometimes the story absolutely depends on the development of that artist's perceptions, as, for example, in *The Ambassadors,* where . . . Strether is transformed in the civilizing atmosphere of Paris. . . . The man who was blind, sees and is saved. . . . for Henry James the good and the beautiful are one. It was all . . . a matter of seeing.

The Girton College lecture gives lyrical development to that idea—as the "artist" reappears:

> . . . consider the universal spirit as a great harmony, unheard by the vast majority of mankind. . . . Here and there someone

stands listening. . . . At a given moment, the listener enters . . . into the creative act and becomes a conductor, able in his degree to change the little twiddlings into something different, more appropriate to the grand symphony.

Bosanquet's work continued to be at the vanguard of James studies, to lead by sane and stellar example. Little of great value had appeared by this time: the magazine *Hound and Horn* had published a collection of essays, "Homage to Henry James," in spring of 1934, as the *Kenyon Review* would in autumn of 1943. When Matthiessen's study of the late novels, *The Major Phase,* was published in 1944, it was the only serious book on James until Elizabeth Stevenson's *The Crooked Corridor* came out in 1949, and then nothing comparable until Frederick Crews' excellent *The Tragedy of Manners* in 1957.

Among Bosanquet's last public performance was her participation in a group interview for the BBC Third Programme on 14 June 1956—"Recollections of Henry James." Her recollections are of secondary importance: she rehearsed her beginning at Lamb House in the "green room," and noted that Mr. James "couldn't bear cut flowers. Never had them in the house." Burgess Noakes added to that his recollection that he and gardener George Gammon used to refer to Mr. James as "the old toff." Of primary importance is the impressive list of co-participants on this occasion: Max Beerbohm, Ruth Draper, Gerard Hopkins, Sir Compton Mackenzie, Ethel Sands, and Peter Warren (son of architect Edward Warren, who introduced James to Lamb House in 1895 and oversaw its renovation for James's occupancy in September 1897). Fond recollections—and in good company.

A final item on Henry James in *Time and Tide* has its own peculiar significance. It is a review of *The House of Fiction; Essays on the Novel,* ed. Leon Edel (4 January 1958, 16–17); an intelligent and complimentary review; its significance is that the author is *not* Theodora Bosanquet but Gerard Hopkins. Something was amiss. *Time and Tide* had been struggling financially for some weeks: the number for 8 March 1958 quite frankly appealed for help (under the byline "Rhondda"). Two weeks later the appeal was repeated (again by the editor, Rhondda); and on 29 March the paper announced "TIME AND TIDE now costs ONE SHILLING"—up from ninepence, a 30% rise. And on 12 April new rates were announced as three pounds (sterling) per annum, which made the shilling weekly rather a minor bargain. Bosanquet was now seventy-eight; Lady Rhondda, three years her junior, had broken her hip in an accident on shipboard early in 1956. They had shared the same address for several years. The issue of *Time and Tide* for Saturday 26 July 1958, announced that "Lady Rhondda died at ten minutes past one last Saturday," that is, 20 July 1958. Time was up; the tide was out.

There remained a final luncheon date for Bosanquet with the burgeoning Jamesian Leon Edel in Chelsea on August 1959. His notes recall their "Chelsea Stroll"—"Cheyney Walk, of course, and Chelsea Old Church (scene of James's funeral), up Lawrence St. to No. 10, where he first took rooms adjacent to Bosanquet and her friend Nellie Bradley." Theodora Bosanquet died on 1 June 1961. Edel added to that reminiscence a firm evaluation of his friendship with "that person whom the other Jameses had mistakenly dismissed as 'little Miss Bosanaquet' and whom I had come to know as a most substantial professional woman and a generous friend."

Theodora Bosanquet was all of that, and an accomplished critic of James's work who anticipated by many years true appreciation of the Master's accomplishment. The last words must be hers; no others could be so timely:

> The essential fact is that wherever he looked Henry James saw fineness apparently sacrificed to grossness, beauty to avarice, truth to a bold front. He realized how constantly the tenderness of growing life is at the mercy of personal tyranny and he hated the tyranny of persons over each other. His novels are a repeated exposure of this wickedness, a reiterated and passionate plea for the fullest freedom of development, unimperilled by reckless and barbarous stupidity.[18]

---

18. See the second-last paragraph of *Henry James at Work*. As I was looking for a conclusion to this little book, something prompted me to turn again the pages of H. Montgomery Hyde's delightful volume *Henry James at Home* (London: Methuen, 1969), which I must have read in the 1970s. (I had met him in 1965, in Rye, during his tenure at Lamb House.) He chose this passage as conclusion to his book. I recognized that I could do no better, and I am pleased to suppose that *mon bon* is still active.

Text design by Mary H. Sexton
Typesetting by Delmastype, Ann Arbor, Michigan
Text face: Perpetua
Type designer Eric Gill's most popular Roman
typeface is Perpetua, which was released by the
Monotype Corporation between 1925 and 1932.
It first appeared in a limited edition of the book
The Passion of Perpetua and Felicity, for which the
typeface was named. The italic form was originally
called Felicity. Perpetua's clean chiseled look recalls
Gill's stonecutting work and makes it an excellent
text typeface, giving sparkle to long passages of
text; the Perpetua capitals have beautiful, classical
lines that make this one of the finest display
alphabets available.
                    —*Courtesy adobe.com*